100ᴜ
Carry On
Film Facts

Brian Carver

Contents

Introduction

The Carry On film comedy series is much loved. With its broad British humour and regular cast members, the Carry Ons were very successful. The films had a low budget, and went through slightly different styles from 1958 to 1992. Some of the films are considered to be among the greatest British films ever made, especially in the comedy genre.

This book of 1000 Carry Facts has trivia on every aspect of the Carry Ons – from the cast, production crew, locations, unmade Carry Ons, anecdotes, behind the scenes stories, the production of the films and much more. Hopefully you will learn something new about this wonderful film (and television!) series.

The Facts

1

There were four television Carry On Christmas specials. They were made by Thames Television.

Carry on Christmas (1969). This is a version of Charles Dickens's A Christmas Carol.

Carry On Again Christmas (1970) is based around the Robert Louis Stevenson story Treasure Island.

Carry On Stuffing (1972) has some historical sketches with an 18th-century banquet as a linking device.

Carry On Christmas (1973) has a series of sketches with a linking device featuring Sid James as a department store Santa.

2

The Carry On films were distributed by Anglo-Amalgamated Productions from 1958 to 1966.

3

Barbara Windsor made ten Carry On films, and Carry On Spying was the only one of these which did not star Sid James.

4

Gail Grainger said she was cast in Carry On Abroad as they wanted someone a bit different and upmarket for the character.

5

All the Carry Ons were made in a planned time period and to a specific budget by Director Gerald Thomas and Producer Peter Rogers so as to be profitable.

6

Carry On Sergeant composer Bruce Montgomery wrote the entire score so it could be played by a military band. It was played by the Band of the Coldstream Guards.

7

The Carry Ons contains the largest number of films of any British film franchise.

8

Richard O' Callaghan appears as the romantic lead in Carry On Loving and Carry On At Your Convenience. He was cast as a replacement for Jim Dale, but he only appears in two Carry Ons.

9

Between 1958 and 1992, there were seven writers of the Carry On films. The two main writers were Norman Hudis (1958–62) and Talbot Rothwell (1963–74).

10

The Carry on films were scored by three different composers: Bruce Montgomery between 1958–62; Eric Rogers between 1963–75 and 1977–78 and Max Harris who scored the 1976 film Carry On England.

11

In 1969 the first Thames Television Carry On Christmas was watched by over eight million viewers.

12

Alexandra Dane understudied Barbara Windsor in the Carry On London stage show.

13

Carry On Sergeant sees Bob Monkhouse's only Carry On role as the leading man.

14

Carry On Nurse was based on the play Ring For Catty by Patrick Cargill and Jack Beal.

15

In the early 2000s, Carry On producer Peter Rogers announced a new Carry On film called Carry On London. The film would be set in a limousine company in London. The director of the British television series The Comic Strip Peter Richardson was named as the director of the new Carry On.

Sets were made at Pinewood studios, but the film did not start production. The project ended after Peter Rogers died in 2008.

16

Carry On Constable was Sid James's first Carry On film.

17

Some other titles for Carry On Jack were:

"Carry On Venus" (Germany), "Beware of the Pirates" (Denmark), "The Mutineers of The Venus" (Belgium) and "Pull Yourself Together Skipper" (Denmark).

18

For his Carry On Constable script, Norman Hudis researched the police at Slough police station. There was a flu outbreak at the station, which Hudis used in his script.

19

Norman Rossington appears in three Carry Ons: Carry On Sergeant, Carry On Nurse and Carry On Regardless.

He also starred in the 1972 TV Christmas special Carry On Stuffing.

20

Carry On Regardless did not have a plot. It consisted of a series of sketches.

21

Joan Sims wrote in her diary that she did not like Carry On At Your Convenience.

22

Liz Fraser appears in four Carry On films: Carry On Regardless Carry On Cruising, Carry On Cabby and Carry On Behind.

23

Michael Pertwee wrote two Carry On film scripts. They were titled Carry on Smoking and Carry On Flying. Smoking was about a fire station. Flying was about an airport.

Carry On producer Peter Rogers decided not to use either script as he was worried about a disaster involving a fire or plane crash would occur during the release of a film based on any of the scripts. Carry On Cruising was made instead.

24

For Carry On Cruising, writer Norman Hudis adapted a short story written by Eric Barker about holidaymakers on a Mediterranean cruise. Eric Barker appears in four Carry On films, but not Cruising.

25

Carry On Columbus cost £2.5 million to make, but only made £1.6 million in the cinema. It made a profit though after a premiere on British satellite channel Sky Movies and from videotape sales.

26

Titles proposed for Carry On At Your Convenience were Carry On Comrade and Carry On Working.

27

Carry On Cabby was bared on a stage play by Dick Hills and Sid Green called Call Me a Cab.

28

Carry On Sergeant was based on a play - The Bull Boys by R. F. Delderfield. The play was about ballet dancers. Writers such as Spike Milligan and Eric Sykes tried to adapt it for a film.

Eventually Norman Hudis wrote a film which became Carry On Sergeant which has members of the army instead of ballet dancers.

29

Carry On Cabby was the first Carry On to feature Jim Dale.

30

Many of the Carry On actors were unhappy with the Carry On clips compilations on British television in the 1980s as they did not receive any repeat fees.

31

Jack Douglas appears in eight Carry On films: Carry On Matron, Carry on Abroad, Carry on Girls, Carry on Dick, Carry on Behind, Carry on England, Carry on Emmannuelle and Carry On Columbus.

He also appears in the 1972 and 1973 Christmas television specials, the Carry On Laughing television series, and the Carry On London and Carry On Laughing stage shows

32

Carry On Jack, the eighth in the series, was the first film of the series to have an historical setting.

33

During the filming of Carry On Camping, poor Terry Scott suffered with hemorrhoids.

34

Before being cast in Carry On Jack, Juliet Mills starred in two other comedies produced by Peter Rogers and directed by Gerald Thomas: Twice Round the Daffodils (1962) and Nurse on Wheels (1963).

35

Carry On Spying was the last Carry On to be filmed in black and white.

36

In 1979, a script for Carry On Again Nurse was written by George Layton and Jonathan Lynn. It was more adult in tone like 1978's Carry On Emmannuelle and the film was not made after Emmannuelle flopped.

37

Carry On producer Peter Rogers registered the Carry On Spying title in 1962 after the first James Bond film Dr No was released in the same year.

38

Robin Askwith appears in one carry On film: Carry On Girls (1973). He plays Larry, the photographer.

39

Carry On Cabby is the first film of the series to be written by Talbot Rothwell. He took two weeks to write the script.

40

For Carry On Cleo, some of the sets and costumes from the 1983 Cleopatra were used. Filming for Cleopatra had started at Pinewood studios - the Carry Ons studio in 1960. But, because of various production difficulties with the big budget film, production on Cleopatra was moved to Rome in 1961.

41

Carry On Cowboy was the first film of the series which featured Peter Butterworth and Bernard Bresslaw.

42

A Carry On film script about amateur actors acting in a production of Romeo and Juliet was written in 1961. The title was What a Carry On...

43

Sid James was unable to appear in Carry On Screaming! as he was revering from a heart attack. His role was taken by Harry H. Corbett.

44

The titles 'Don't Shoot 'til you See the Whites of their Thighs' and 'The Lust Continent' were unused credit titles for Carry On Up the Jungle.

45

Dilys Laye was allowed by producer Peter Rogers to keep the outfits she wore in Carry On Camping, such as the green and pink dress she wears in the cinema scene.

46

In 1966 Nat Cohen took over Carry On producer Anglo Amalgamated Film Distributors Ltd as managing director. Cohen did not like the Carry On series. As a result the Carry Ons had to move to Rank to distribute the films.

47

Lance Peters was credited as the screenwriter for Carry On Emmannuelle. Peter Rogers, Willy Rushton and Vince Powell added dialogue, but were un-credited.

48

In Carry On Camping, Miss Haggard (Hattie Jacques) wears a blue towel on her head during the scene where Babs's bra flies off. The towel disappears and reappears during the scene.

49

Carry On Follow That Camel was based loosely on the P.C. Wren novel Beau Geste. Beau Geste is a novel written in 1924 about English brothers who enlist in the French Foreign Legion.

50

A double ententre is a phrase which has two meanings: a phrase can be innocent but also have a sexual meaning. The Carry On films are famous for their double ententres.

51

Phil Silvers was paid £40,000 to appear in Carry On Follow That Camel. This was the biggest fee any actor was paid in the series.

52

Carry On Doctor was intended to be the last film in the series.

53

Joan Sims played a stern Matron in Doctor in Clover and was going to play the Matron role In Carry On Doctor. But traditional Carry On matron Hattie Jacques got the role.

54

Bette Davis was making a film at Pinewood at the same time as Carry On Abroad was being filmed. At one stage some of the Carry On actors were messing around in the makeup room. Davis was in a neighbouring dressing room and she told then off for disturbing her.

55

Carry On Doctor was the first film to have illustrations by Larry in the opening credits.

56

Filmed on location in Snowdonia, North Wales, Carry On Up the Khyber was the only film to have scenes filmed outside England; scene were filmed in Wales.

57

Terence Longdon appeared in four of the first five Carry On films, before leaving as he did not want to be "pigeon holed".

Later in life he said the stars of the series were great comedians, whereas he was "just a proper actor".

58

It took three days to film the final dinner scene in Carry On Up the Khyber.

59

Carry On Camping was at number one in the UK box office when released.

60

Norman Mitchell appears in five Carry On films: Carry On Spying, Carry On Screaming, Carry On Emmannuelle, Carry On Cabby and Carry On Cleo.

61

Carry On Again Doctor was the last Carry On to feature Jim Dale.

62

In the 1980s, Carry On actor Jack Douglas wrote a Carry On script called Carry On Parliament. But, the political themed Carry On was never made.

63

In Carry On Again Doctor, soundtrack composer Eric Rogers has a cameo as trumpet player during the hospital dance scene.

64

In Carry On Constable, when Sgt. Wilkins and P.C. Thurston go on patrol in the police car, the registration number changes between scenes: from 892FPC to UUV133.

65

Frankie Howard's part as Dr Tinkle in Carry On Up The Jungle was written for Kenneth Williams.

66

Talbot Rothwell originally titled his Carry On Loving script Carry On Courting.

67

Carry On Henry was going to be called Anne of a Thousand Lays - a pun on the film Anne of the Thousand Days (1969).

68

The Carry Ons were self contained films: there were no sequels or continuing plots over multiple films.

69

Carry On Girls is the first Carry On which did not have either Kenneth Williams and Charles Hawtrey in it.

70

Carry On at Your Convenience was known as Carry On Round the Bend in countries outside Britain.

71

In order to receive an A certificate from the British censors, a few lines were removed from Carry On Up the Khyber. These were: Brother Belcher (Peter Butterworth) asking for "a tool to dig with" and Bungdit Din (Bernard Bresslaw) talking about a "travelling fakir".

72

Carry On At Your Convenience (released in 1971) did not make a profit until 1976 after international and television profits.

73

Carry On Matron was the last medical-based film in the Carry On series.

74

Norman Hudis was asked to write a script for Carry On Matron. Hudis had written the early Carry On films.

Unfortunately he was living in the US and a member of the Writers Guild Of America which created difficulties for him writing a film script in Britain.

75

Carry On Matron was the first film to feature Jack Douglas.

76

The Carry On humour is very like that of the traditional British music hall.

The Music Hall is a British stage tradition involving variety entertainment such as often bawdy songs and comedy, and variety acts such as magicians and acrobats.

Popular between 1850 and 1960, elements of the Music Hall tradition influenced the Carry On film. Carry On screenwriter Talbot Rothwell was a big fan of the risqué music hall comedian Max Miller.

77

Carry On Abroad was Charles Hawtrey's last Carry On.

78

During the filming of Carry On Doctor, Kenneth Williams recorded his radio programme Stop Messing About on Monday mornings.

79

Kenneth Williams was unavailable for Carry On Girls due to appearing in the theatre. A smaller role was offered to him but he could not appear in the film. The role went to Jimmy Logan.

80

Carry On writer Talbot Rothwell was considering leaving his role after Carry on Girls. The producers asked Lawrie Wyman and George Evans to write a script for the next Carry On. They wrote a Dick Turpin themed script.

Rothwell did return as the writer and adapted the script as Carry On Dick. Wyman and Evans received an acknowledgment for the plot in the credits.

81

That's Carry On! was co-produced by EMI.

82

Carry On Constable was the first Carry On to turn Charles Hawtrey's first appearance as a special moment, with his "Oh, hello!" phrase.

83

Elke Sommer was paid £30,000 to play the Roman expert Anna Vooshka in Carry On Behind.

84

The idea for Carry On England was written as a script by David Pursell and Jack Seddon for an episode entitled The Busting of Balsy for the Carry On Laughing television series in 1975.

The Carry On producers decided to use the script for Carry On England instead.

85

Liz Fraser was not cast by producer Peter Rogers in Carry Ons after carry On Cabby in 1963 after criticising the marketing of the films to Stuart Levy, the head of Carry On distributor Anglo-Amalgamated. She did return for Carry On Behind in 1975.

86

Sid James had said he was not available for Carry On England as he was appearing in The Mating Season stage play. Sadly, Sid died a month before Carry On England started filming.

87

Joan Sims and Kenneth Williams fell out on the set of Carry On Screaming! after Kenneth was rude to Joan's guests who were visiting the set.

88

The idea for the Carry On compilation That's Carry On! came Metro-Goldwyn-Mayer's popular compilation film That's Entertainment! (1974). That's Entertainment! is a compilation of clips from classic MGM musical films.

89

Harry Enfield, a big fan of the Carry Ons was offered the role of Bart Columbus in Carry On Columbus. But he did not think the film would work after the death of so many Carry On stars and turned down the role.

90

Talbot Rothwell struggled during writing the Carry On Dick script suffering from nervous exhaustion.

91

In Carry On Girls, Mrs Dukes's knickers are hoisted on Madeira Drive in Brighton.

92

Dr. Nookey's (Jim Dale) clinic in Carry On Again doctor is located on Park Street in Windsor, Berkshire.

93

Australian author Lance Peters provided the script for Carry On Emmannuelle.

94

Sidney James's daughter Sue James appears as a little girl in Carry On Constable.

95

The dresses worn by Dilys Laye in Carry On Cruising were bought in London's West End. Laye was allowed to keep the outfits.

96

Norman Hudis wrote the first six Carry On films and they are more sentimental in tone than the other films in the series.

97

The term Carry On came from the first film Carry On Sergeant. Carry On is phrase used by an officer when handing over a parade or inspection to an NCO. An American equivalent is As You Were.

98

Tommy Cooper, the famous Welsh comedian, was offered the part of the fakir (played by Cardew Robinson) in Carry On Up The Khyber.

99

Frank Thornton has one role in a Carry On - in Carry On Screaming as the shopkeeper.

100

The co-producer at Anglo-Amalgamated was not keen in the title The Bull Boys, the play on which Carry On Sergeant was based. He suggested Carry On Sergeant, inspired by Anglo-Amalgamated's 1957 film Carry On Admiral.

101

Peter Butterworth was a prisoner of war during World War 2, in the German Stalag Luft III camp in Poland with Carry On screenwriter Talbot Rothwell. Butterworth helped plan the escape that was made into the film The Great Escape (1963).

102

Fenella Fielding appears in two Carry On films.

103

Snogging on-the-Green train station in Carry On Loving is Windsor Central train station.

104

Singer and actor David Essex had his small role cut from Carry On Henry.

105

Carry On Nurse was the top-grossing film of 1959 in Britain.

106

Gerald Thomas gained royal permission to film Carry On

Henry in the grounds of Windsor Castle, which was the first time a film had been granted such permission.

107

Bernard Bresslaw had an unedited role in Carry On Nurse. His feet were used standing in a bath! He was a stand in for Terence Longdon

108

Kenneth Williams received £800 for Carry On Sergeant. The average annual wage in Britain in 1958 was £250.

109

A British comedy film called Carry On Admiral was made in 1957. It is similar to the earlier Carry On's and stars Joan Sims, but has no connection to the Carry On series.

110

Carry On Teacher was filmed at Drayton Green Primary School, Ealing, London.

111

Carry On Constable, released in 1960, was Leslie Phillips's last Carry On for 32 years.

112

In an interview Peter Rogers was asked about the new team of electricians and carpenters working behind on the set of Carry On Columbus [on the earlier Carry Ons, he would have many of the same electricians and carpenters]. He replied: "I'm not a fan, and I find them noisy and vulgar. The Carry On's may heave been rude, but never vulgar. It's the difference between shit and treading in it."

113

A 2007 poll of 1000 comic writers, comedians and comedy club owner to find the funniest movie one liner of all time named a Carry On line as number one.: "infamy, infamy, they've all got it infamy" said by Kenneth Williams in Carry On Cleo was number one.

114

Carry On Constable was the third most popular film at the British box office in 1960. Doctor in Love and Sink the Bismarck! were the top two.

115

Joan Sims became ill shortly before filming began on Carry On Cruising. She was replaced by Dilys Laye.

116

Charles Hawtrey was not cast in Carry On Cruising as he demanded top billing. He returned in the next Carry On - Cabby.

117

Deborah Kerr was initially offered the role of Valeria Watt in Carry On Screaming; she turned down the role.

118

Australian actor Vincent Ball appears in two Carry Ons; in Carry On Cruising as Jenkins and Carry On Follow That Camel as Ship's Officer.

119

Liz Fraser makes her third consecutive third appearance in Carry On Cabby in 1963. Her fourth Carry On appearance is 12 years later in Carry On Behind.

120

Jim Dale complained about the working conditions on the set of Carry On Screaming!, which angered producer Peter Rogers.

121

Carry On Spying parodies various spy films of the period, which were very popular. The films parodied include The Third Man (1949), and the then new James Bond series.

122

Shirley Eaton appears in three early Carry On films. She wasn't able to return for Carry On Teacher as she was pregnant. She retired from acting in 1969 to concentrate on family life.

123

In June 2008 the Royal Mail in Britain released stamps with the posters of Carry On Cleo, Carry On Sergeant and Carry On

Screaming! On them. They were released as a celebration of the 50th anniversary of the Carry On series.

124

The original poster for Carry On Cleo was withdrawn after a copyright case. Tom Chantrell had created the artwork and based it on a painting by Howard Terpning. 20th Century Fox sued Carry On distributor as they said they owned the copyright for the Terpning painting.

125

The exterior of the police station in Carry On Constable is Hanwell Library, Cherrington Road, London.

126

In 2018, the British Film Institute wrote a retrospective of the Cary On films and named their top five films. They were Carry On Cleo, Carry On Screaming, Carry On Up The Khyber, Carry On Camping and Carry On Matron.

127

The Rocky Horror Picture Show creator and The Crystal Maze host Richard O'Brien as an uncredited role in Carry On Cowboy as a horse rider.

128

Carry On Cowboy is the first film in the series to have song with vocals in the title sequence. Ballads in the title sequence were common in westerns.

129

Valeria Watt in Carry On Screaming! is a parody of Morticia Addams from The Addams Family.

130

Lance Percival stood in for Charles Hawtrey in Carry On Cruising playing the ship's chef.

131

The cars used for the Glamcabs in Carry On Cabby were Ford Cortinas. These were new cars from Ford that were first sold in September 1962. Ford used Carry On Cabby to advertise the Cortina.

132

Sydney Bromley was going to play Dan Dann in Carry On Screaming! in what was going to be a minor role. But, distributors in the US wanted Charles Hawtrey in the film as he was very popular with American audiences. So Hawtrey played Dan Dann in Carry On Screaming!.

133

In the 1980s, Carry On Dallas, a spoof of the American television drama Dallas, was planned. Vince Powell wrote the script, and Carry On stars such as Kenneth Williams were signed up. But, the film was scrapped. One reason given was that Dallas producers Lorimar wanted a large royalty fee.

134

In 1959, Carry On distributor Stuart Levy had an idea for a Carry On about the Church of England. Director Gerald Thomas made a tongue in cheek remark that a Carry On making fun of the Church of England would be in bad taste. This was because Gerald Thomas, Peter Rogers and Stuart Levy were all Jewish!

135

Carry On director Gerald Thomas is the voice of Oddbod Junior in Carry On Screaming! in an uncredited role.

136

Phil Silvers as Sergeant Nocker plays a similar character his Sergeant Bilko character in Carry On Follow That Camel. Army Sergeant Bilko appears in the popular US sitcom The Phil Silvers Show which ran from 1955-1959.

137

The nudist film that is seen in the cinema in Carry On Camping is Nudist Paradise (1959).

138

Carry On Doctor made the third largest amount of money in British cinemas in 1968. The Jungle Book and Barbarella were the top two in the box office list.

139

Hugh Futcher appears in seven Carry On films: Carry On

Spying, Carry On Abroad Carry On At Your Convenience, Carry On Behind, Carry On Don't Lose Your Head, Carry On Again Doctor and Carry On Girls.

140

Terry Scott had a small role in the first Carry On film, Carry On Sergeant, in 1958. He returned in 1968 for Carry On Up The Khyber, the 16th in the series.

141

Two Carry On films have "Up The" in the title: Carry On Up The Khyber (1968) and Carry On Up The Jungle (1970).

Frankie Howerd - star of Carry On Up The Jungle appears in a trio of related films, one with Up in the title and two with Up The in the title. They are Up Pompeii (1971), Up The Chasity Belt (1972) and Up The Front (1972). Up Pompeii in a film version of the television series created by Carry On scriptwriter Talbot Rothwell. In Up The Chasity Belt Howerd plays the same character as in Up Pompeii, but this time set in 12th Century England. The third Up The Front again has Howerd playing the same character during World War 1.

142

After Carry On Nurse was a hit producer Peter Rogers decided to make several more Carry Ons. He offered the Carry On regulars a percentage of the takings instead of a flat fee. The actors took the flat fee.

143

The pith helmets worn in Carry On Up The Khyber were those

used in the 1964 war film Zulu.

144

Joan Sims last Carry On film appearance was in Carry On Emmannuelle in 1978. she was paid £2500 - the same fee she earnt in her first Carry On, Carry On Nurse.

145

In September 2005, a plaque was unveiled in Snowdonia in North Wales to mark the spot of where Carry On Up The Khyber was filmed.

146

Carry On Girls was not a success at the British box office. This led to the Carry On Christmas television specials being cancelled.

147

Peter Rogers produced every Carry On film and Gerald Thomas directed every film in the series.

148

The cinema in Carry On Camping is the Everyman Cinema in Gerrards Cross, Buckinghamshire. This famous old cinema dating back to 1925 is still there.

149

There were three films released in 1992 to commemorate the 500th anniversary of Christopher Columbus's landing in

America. Christopher Columbus: The Discovery, 1492: Conquest of Paradise and a Carry On - Carry On Columbus. All three films were not a success, but Carry On Columbus made more money in the British cinemas than the other two films.

150

French actress Dany Robin appears in Carry On Don't Lose Your Head. She was married to agent Michael Sullivan, who was Sid James's agent. Unfortunately, Robin and Sullivan died in an apartment fire in Paris in 1995.

151

Talbot Rothwell's original Carry On Again Doctor script caused some legal problems as the story featuring a medical mission and slimming pill was similar to a script Rothwell had submitted for the Doctor series of films. But Doctor film producer Betty Box had not taken up an option on the script so it was able to used for the Carry On film.

152

Bernard Bresslaw appears in fourteen of the Carry On films:

Carry On Cowboy, Carry On Screaming, Carry On Follow That Camel, Carry On Doctor, Carry On Up the Khyber, Carry On Camping, Carry On Up the Jungle, Carry On Loving, Carry On at Your Convenience, Carry On Matron, Carry On Abroad, Carry On Girls, Carry On Dick, and Carry On Behind.

Bresslaw also performed in the Carry On London and What A Carry On in Blackpool stage productions.

He starred in the 1969, 1970, and 1973 Christmas television

specials, and the Carry On Laughing television series.

153

In Carry On Spying, Kenneth Williams's character was based on his snide persona he used in radio shows such as Hancock's Half Hour.

154

Some of the alternative titles for Carry On At Your Convenience are:

"A Dangerous Strike" (Germany), "Carry On Your Way" (Hungary) and "How Do You Make Your Bed" (Poland).

155

There was a possibility that Sid James would not be able to appear in Carry On Henry as he was appearing on stage in South Africa. But, James cut short his theatre work to appear in Henry.

156

Carry On composer Eric Rogers did not compose the score for Carry On England. This is because cuts to the budget resulted in the orchestra being cut from 40 to 20 musicians and as a result Rogers did not to work on the film. Rogers returned for Carry On Emmannelle.

157

Victor Maddern appears in five Carry On films: Carry On Constable, Carry On Regardless, Carry On Spying, Carry On

Cleo and Carry On Emmannuelle.

He also appeared in three episodes of the Carry On Laughing television series.

158

The interior scenes for Carry On Girls were filmed at Pinewood studios.

159

When Sid eats his ice lolly in the cinema in Carry On Camping, the size of the lolly keeps changing.

160

In a 2018 retrospective on the series, the British Film Institute named the five worst Carry On films. They were: Carry On Girls, Carry On England, That's Carry On!, Carry On Emmannuelle, and Carry On Columbus.

161

In Carry On Behind, Joan Sims plays Patsy Rowland's mother. She was only eight months older than Rowlands.

162

Farce is a type of comedy. It portrays comic situations that are exaggerated and improbable. Physical comedy, misunderstandings, one liners and innuendo are heavily used in the plot.

The word farce comes from the French word for stuffing.

Farce was used in 15th century to lampoon religious and political affairs. It is a gentler, less serious criticism than satire.

Examples of British farce plays, television and theatre include - William Shakespeare: The Comedy of Errors (c. 1592), Oscar Wilde: The Importance of Being Earnest (1895), Joe Orton What the Butler Saw (1969) BBC sitcom, Fawlty Towers (1975).

Farce is still a popular form in the theatre. The Carry On series has many elements of traditional farce with its stereotypical characters, lampooning of British institutions and society, innuendo and humour based on misunderstanding and bizarre situations.

163

In the 2011 Time Out List of the 100 Greatest Comedies of All Time, Carry On Screaming came in at 99

164

Larry - real name Terence Parkes - was an English cartoonist.

He drew the distinctive and risque credit cartoons for Carry On Doctor, Carry On up the Khyber Carry on Camping and Carry On Girls.

He worked was published in many publications, such as Punch and Private Eye.

Larry's style was absurdist and minimalist.

165

Johnny Briggs, Mike Baldwin in British soap opera Coronation Street, has a role in Carry On Behind in an uncredited role as a plasterer.

166

Julian Holloway appears in eight Carry On films:

Carry On Follow That Camel, Carry On Doctor, Carry On Up the Khyber, Carry On Camping, Carry On Loving, Carry On Henry, Carry On at Your Convenience, and Carry On England.

167

The hall where Francis Biggar holds his lecture in Carry On Doctor is the Old Masonic Temple, New Windsor Street in Uxbridge. The building is an apartment block.

168

That's Carry On! was released in 1977 as a supporting feature to the Richard Harris film, Golden Rendezvous. Golden Rendezvous is based on an Alistair MacLean novel and is an action film about a nuclear bomb on a cruise liner. It flopped at the box office.

169

The 1953 horror film House of Wax, starring Vincent Price, has a similar plot to Carry On Screaming! Both films have young women being abducted and encased in wax.

170

Film critic Philip French wrote this in his review of Carry On Emmannuelle:

"This relentless sequence of badly-written, badly-timed dirty jokes is surely one of the most morally and aesthetically offensive pictures to emerge from a British studio".

171

Bill Maynard appears in five Carry On films:

Carry On Loving, Carry On Henry, Carry On At Your Convenience, Carry On Matron and Carry On Dick.

172

When the first Gulf War started in 1990, Carry On Up the Khyber was one of he films banned from British television.

173

Norman Hudis and Talbot Rothwell both wrote scripts for Carry On Spying. Rothwell's script was used.

174

The first shot in the Carry On films is of St Mary and All Saints Church, Beaconsfield, Buckinghamshire (in Carry On Sergeant).

175

Carry On Spying had some of these alternative titles:

"Agent Oooh!" (Europe), "Carry On Espionage" (Hungary), "Agent Secret 0.0.0.H! against Dr. Crow" (Belgium) and "Watch out for the Spies" (South America).

176

Carry On Jack was going to be a separate film from the series. It was made into a Carry On after its original title, Up The Armada, was considered to be too rude by the British Board of Film Censors.

177

Jim Dale and Sid James came up with thee 'Drop in in the basket' line that Charles Hawtrey says when he's at the guillotine in Carry On Don't Lose Your Head.

178

The poster for Carry On Spying parodied the artwork for the James films From Russia With Love (1963).

179

One key part of the humour of the Carry Ons is the pun. A pun is a humorous use of a word or phrase that has several meanings, or that sounds like another word.

An example is this pun from Carry On Matron:

Matron: I'm a simple woman with simple tastes, and I want to be wooed.

Bernard: Oh you can be as wude as you like with me!

180

The Police Station in Carry On Constable is Hanwell library on Cherington Road in Ealing, London.

181

Carry On cinematographer Alan Hume did not work on Carry On Up the Khyber as he thought the title was crude. He believed the Carry On series was starting to become more risque and rude. Later in his autobiography he said he had made a mistake as he thought Carry On Up the Khyber was the best Carry On.

182

For Carry On Girls, June Whitfield (Augusta Prodworthy in the film) dubbed Valerie Leon's voice. In an interview with Carry On Whitfield says she could not remember dubbing Leon's voice, and no one seems to know why Leon's voice was dubbed.

183

Francis Courtney (Kenneth Williams) walks along with the chimp in Carry On Regardless on Clarence Crescent, in Windsor, Berkshire.

184

Kenneth Williams was originally going to play Francis Bigger in Carry On Doctor. But, he did not like the character so was given the Dr Tinkle role. Bigger was played by Frankie Howerd.

185

Bill Kenwright, the theatre producer and former Chairman of English football club Everton, plays a reporter in Carry On Matron.

186

In Carry On Cabby, Charlie drops the newly married couple off at Terminal Three at Heathrow Airport, London.

187

Bill Owen appears in four Carry On films: Carry On Sergeant (1958), Carry On Nurse (1959), Carry On Regardless (1961) and Carry On Cabby (1963).

188

In Carry On Doctor, Hattie Jacques and Amita Harris are billed ninth and tenth. They also have big parts in the film. Barbara Windsor is the highest billed female star, nut has a smaller role than Jacques and Harris. Barbara is also only making her second Carry On appearance.

189

Peter Rogers said Carry On Up The Khyber was his favourite Carry On film.

190

Producer Peter Rogers and director Gerald Thomas made several other non Carry On film comedies together. These comedies were very similar to the Carry On films, and featured many Carry On actors and other crew:

Please Turn Over (1959)

Directed by Gerald Thomas

Produced by Peter Rogers

Written by Norman Hudis
Music by Bruce Montogomery

Stars: Ted Ray, Leslie Phillips, Jean Kent, Joan Sims, Charles Hawtrey, Dilys Laye, Marianne Stone.

A 17 year old girl writes a fictional book about the secrets of her family and the residents of her town. Many of the residents mistakenly think the book is a real life account.

The film is a pleasant late 50s British farce with the expected charm. It has a great ensemble cast too.

Watch Your Stern (1960)

Directed by Gerald Thomas

Produced by Peter Rogers

Written by Earle Couttie and Alan Hackney.
Music by Bruce Montgomery

Stars: Eric Barker. Leslie Phillips, Kenneth Connor, Sid James, Hattie Jacques. Spike Milligan and Joan Sims.

The film is set on a British warship: the HMS Terrier. The crew lose the plans for a secret weapon. An Admiral wants to show them to a scientist, so the crew have to pretend they still have the plans.

This is a very pleasant gentle farce, typical of the British comedy films of the era.

Raising the Wind (1961)

Directed by Gerald Thomas

Produced by Peter Rogers

Written by Bruce Montgomery

Music by Edmund Crispin

Stars: James Robertson Justice, Leslie Phillips, Paul Massie, Kenneth Williams, Liz Fraser, Sid James, Lance Percival, Jim Dale.

The film is about a group of students at a London music school.

It's a fun farce with a selection of familiar Carry On faces. It similar to the Doctor films and even has Doctor star James Robertson Justice as the authority figure.

Nurse on Wheels (1963)

Directed by Gerald Thomas

Produced by Peter Rogers

Written by Norman Hudis

Music by Eric Rogers

Stars: Juliet Mills, Ronald Lewis, Joan Sims, Esmee Cannon. Noel Purcell, Renee Houston, Jim Dale.

Nurse Joanna Jones (Juliet Mills) takes on a job as a district nurse in the countryside visiting patients in their homes.

Nurse On Wheels is a gentle comedy drama from the Carry On production team. It does not have as many Carry On regulars as some of the other comedies from Thomas and Rogers.

The Big Job (1965)

Directed by Gerald Thomas

Produced by Peter Rogers and Frank Bevis

Written by Talbot Rothwell and John Antrobus

Music by Eric Rogers

Stars: Sid James, Dick Emery, Joan Sims, Syvia Syms, Jim Dale, Lance Percival.

A gang of robbers, led by George Brain (Sid James) steal £50000 in 1950. He hides the money in the trunk of a hollow tree in the countryside before him and his gang are caught. In 1965 they are released from prison. The go to retrieve the money, only to find that a new town has been built on the countryside, and the tree with the money is tn the yard of a police station. The gang rent a room in a house across the road from the police station an attempt to get the money.

A very entertaining Carry On-esque comedy with an

interesting cast, led by Sid James. Nice exteriors with the contemporary new town locations too.

Bless This House (1972)

Directed by Gerald Thomas

Produced by Peter Rogers

Written by Dave Freeman

Music by Eric Rogers

Stars: Sid James, Diana Coupland, Terry Scott, June Whitfield, Peter Butterworth, Sally Geeson, Robin Askwith and Patsy Rowlands

Sid Abbott (Sid James) lives in the suburbs wife his wife and two children. He does not get on with new neighbour Ronald Baines (Terry Scott), which leads to problems when Sid's son and Ronald's daughter start a romance.

Bless This House is an entertaining adaption of the popular sitcom. The film has some amusing sketches with Sid the traditional office worker Sid battling his environmentalist daughter, art student son and wife who has become obsessed with selling antiques.

191

Sir Rodney Ffing's Manor House In Carry On Don't Lose Your Head is Cliveden House, an Italianite mansion in Buckinghamshire.

192

Some alternative titles for Carry On Behind are:

"Everything Backfires" (West Germany), "The Wacky Campers" (Denmark), "Carry On Digging" (Hungary), "A Taste of Honey" (Turkey), "Camping Cheerleader" (Italy) and "Now We take the Romans" (Sweden).

193

Kenneth Williams appears in twenty-six Carry films:

Carry On Sergeant, Carry On Nurse, Carry On Teacher, Carry On Constable, Carry On Regardless, Carry On Cruising, Carry On Jack, Carry On Spying, Carry On Cleo, Carry On Cowboy, Carry On Screaming, Carry On Don't Lose Your Head (1966), Carry On Follow That Camel, Carry On Doctor, Carry On Up the Khyber, Carry On Camping, Carry On Again Doctor, Carry On Loving, Carry On Henry, Carry On at Your Convenience, Carry On Matron, Carry On Abroad, Carry On Dick, Carry On Behind, That's Carry On!, and Carry On Emmannuelle.

194

The Carry Ons were filmed in Britain for budgetary reasons. Also, apparently producer Peter Rogers had a "phobia of foreign travel".

195

Carry On At Sea was a proposed title for Carry On Cruising.

196

Angela Douglas's Carry On films were all historical: Carry On Cowboy (1965), Carry on Screaming (1966), Carry on Follow That Camel (1967) and Carry On Up The Khyber (1967).

197

The Helter Skelter in Carry On At Your Convenience is on the Palace Pier - now Brighton Pier - in Brighton.

198

The Potters' house in Carry On Camping is in Pinewood Close, near Pinewood Studios.

199

Valerie Leon appears in six Carry On films:

Carry On Up The Khyber, Carry On Camping, Carry On Again Doctor, Carry On Up The Jungle, Carry On Matron and Carry On Girls.

Also appeared in Carry On Christmas 1972.

200

Carry On Don't Lose Your Head and Carry On Follow That Camel were both released without the Carry On title.

The Carry On title was abandoned after a distribution deal with Rank. The two films were re-released with the Carry On titles and box office taking increased. Distributors Rank allowed the Carry On title to be used for future films.

201

Chayste Place in Carry On Camping is Heatherden Hall in Pinewood studios.

202

Fenella Fielding turned down a role in Carry On Cleo as she was on holiday in New York.

203

Frankie Howerd appears in two Carry On films, Carry On Doctor and Carry Up the Jungle.

He also appeared in the Carry On Christmas television special in 1969.

204

Sir Michael Caine's wife, Lady Shakira Caine, appears in Carry On Again Doctor.

205

Rank did not want to provide all the funding for Carry On England. Peter Rogers and Gerald Thomas had to fund part of the film.

206

The interior scenes of the nursing Home in Carry On Again Doctor were filmed in Heatherden Hall in Pinewood Studios.

207

With Carry On Emmannuelle, producer Peter Rogers wanted to copy the British sex comedies of the Confessions of... series which were very popular in Britain in the 1970s.

208

In 1961, Carry On writer Norman Hudis came up with an idea for a Carry On based in a fire station. His idea for the title was Carry On Smoking. Producer Peter Rogers did not like the idea, and was concerned that a fire disaster would occur during the film's release.

209

The Carry On Sergeant army camp exterior scenes were filmed at Cardwell's Keep, Stoughton Barracks, Stoughton Road, Stoughton, Guildford, Surrey.

210

The filming of Carry On Cabby is portrayed in the 2011 BBC drama Hattie, a dramatisation of the life of Hattie Jacques. Ruth Jones plays Hattie.

211

The Wedded Bliss Agency in Carry On Loving is located on the corner of Park Street and Sheet Street in Windsor, Berkshire.

212

Hattie Jacques plays her famous Matron Carry on character in five Carry Ons.

In Carry On Nurse she plays the Matron.

In Carry On Doctor she plays the Matron.

In Carry On Camping she plays the school's Matron Miss Haggerd.

In Carry On Again Doctor she makes another appearance as the Matron.

Carry On Matron sees her play the Matron of the maternity hospital.

213

Talbot Rothwell wrote a script for a Carry On about British soldiers in a German prisoner of war camp in World War 2. Titled Carry On Escaping, it was a spoof of World War 2 prison escape films. Rothwell had been in a German POW camp during World War 2 with Peter Butterworth. It was considered for a 1973 release, but sadly never made.

214

The Parkway Hotel Cocktail Bar in Carry On Loving is in the Ye Hearte and Garter Hotel in Windsor.

215

In Carry On Behind, Barnes (Peter Butterworth) writes Men on the shower block in small letters. Later on the writing is much bigger.

216

Rogerham Mansions in Carry On Loving is opposite Atherton Court in Eton, Berkshire.

217

There is a common belief that Carry On Cleo used sets built for Cleopratra (1963). But, Carry On Cleo's cinematographer, Alan Hume, said that Carry On Cleo used specifically designed sets deigned by the film's art director Bert Davey.

218

Carry On Up the Khyber was voted 99th in the British Film Institute's poll of the finest 100 films ever made in the 20th Century. This poll was conducted in 1999. The British Film Institute asked 1000 people from British film and television.

219

Some alternative titles for Carry On England are:

"Mixed Barracks" (Italy), "Now we take England" (Sweden), "Saviour of the Nation" (Germany), "Lets Go England" (Finland), and "Way to Go . . . England" (Portugal).

220

In Carry On Henry, King Henry VIII and his companions ride down the Long Walk at Windsor Castle.

221

Comedy writer Vince Powell suggested a new modern format

for the Carry Ons in the 1980s under the title of Tales of...

222

In 1961, a Carry On about the space race was written. Norman Hudis wrote a script in 1961 called Carry On Spaceman. It satirised the space race between the USA and the Soviet Union; the plot saw three incompetent British astronauts sent into space.

223

Julian Holloway said he was critical of the Carry On series in the Carry On Forever television documentary. But his criticisms were edited out.

224

Vic Spanners House in Carry On At Your Convenience was the Baker Street set originally constructed for the Sherlock Holmes film The Private Life of Sherlock Holmes (1970).

225

The final shot of Carry On Sergeant was filmed at the entrance to Pinewood Studios.

226

Anthony Sagar had his part of a heckler in Carry On Henry deleted from the final film.

227

The opening credit music for Carry On Screaming! was

released in 1996 as a 45rpm vinyl. The record was sung by Boz Burell. The film version was sung by a different singer - Ray Pilgrim.

228

Carol Hawkins appears in two Carry On films: Carry On Abroad and Carry On Behind.

She also appears in two episodes of the Carry On Laughing television series.

229

Hattie Jacques appears in fourteen Carry On films:

Carry On Sergeant, Carry On Nurse, Carry On Teacher, Carry On Constable, Carry On Regardless, Carry On Cabby, Carry On Doctor, Carry On Camping, Carry On Again Doctor, Carry On Loving, Carry On at Your Convenience, Carry On Matron, Carry On Abroad and Carry On Dick.

230

Finisham Maternity Hospital in Carry On Matron is is Heatherwood Maternity Hospital in Ascot, Berkshire.

231

In Carry On At Your Convenience, Sid Plummer (Sid James) wins money betting on horses and buys anew car. He replaces his Ford 100E car with a Morris Marina 1.3 Deluxe Coupe in Bedouin. This car was a new model when the film was shot.

232

In Carry On Matron, the marriage takes place at Denham Church, Denham, Buckinghamshire.

233

In Carry On Abroad, The Wundatours office is on the High Street in Slough, Berkshire.

234

During the filming of Carry On Up the Khyber, Princess Margaret visited the set. She was shown the clip in which Sir Sidney writes to Queen Victoria and writes "Dear Vicky". Princess Margaret was angered by calling Victoria Vicky.

235

In Carry On Girls the shelter where the family take cover from the rain is located in Madeira Drive in Brighton.

236

In the scene in Carry On Camping where Bernie pours water on Sid by accident, Sid moves his head so the water falls on him.

237

Lance Percival was paid £600 for his role in Carry On Cruising. This meant the producers saved money, as Percival replaced Charles Hawtrey in the film: Hawtrey would have received £4000.

238

In 1937 a British crime film was made called Carry On London. It has no connection to the Carry On series.

239

Fircombe Mayor Frederick Bumble's house in Carry On Girls is on Lansdowne Avenue in Slough.

240

Carry On Emmannuelle was not distributed by Rank. Producer Peter Rogers managed to obtain a £349000 investment in the film from private investment company Cleves Investments.

241

When Kenneth Williams was filming Carry On Sergeant, he was also appearing in London at the Garrick Theatre in the West End revue Share My Lettuce.

242

In Carry On Girls, Sid escapes on a go kart on Brighton's West Pier. The West Pier was closed in 1975 and has eroded over the years despite attempts to restore it.

243

The Church in Carry On Dick is St Mary's Church, Hitcham, Buckinghamshire.

244

There is one Carry On television series of thirteen episodes. It is called Carry On Laughing.

The episodes were broadcast between 4th January 1975 and 7th December 1975. The series was made by ATV. The episodes parodied famous books, play and films.

245

King Charles III visited the Carry On Cabby set aged 14.

246

In Carry On Nurse, the outdoor scenes of the patients walking around were filmed in the gardens at Pinewood.

247

In Carry On Cleo, Jim Dale's character attacks some Romans and then flees. Sidney James (Mark Antony) arrives and sees Kenneth Connor (Hengist) is dazed with a sword, and collapses. Sid says "What a carve up!". Kenneth Connor and Sid James previously starred in murder mystery comedy What a Carve Up! (1961).

248

Fred Ramsden's butchers shop in Carry On Behind is on Robin Parade in Farnham Common.

249

Shirley Eaton appears in three Carry On films - Carry On

Sergeant, Carry On Nurse and Carry On Constable.

250

Peter Rogers was worried that Frankie Howerd's personality would "clash" with the cast in Carry On Up the Jungle. Howerd sent a letter to Rogers saying he would adapt to the film:

"This is to reassure you that no such thing will happen. Believe me, I know well your attitudes to work, time schedules and shooting – thus, once I am agreed to be an employee of yours I would naturally expect to abide by all the rules. So now, stop worrying and put a bottle of champagne on ice!"

251

In Carry On Behind, Fred and Ernie leave to go to the campsite and drive down the High Street in Farnham Common, Buckinghamshire.

252

For Carry On Cabby, Charles Hawtrey had to be taught how to drive. He had one week to learn and passed his test a few days before filming started.

253

The entrance to the Camp in Carry On England is on Pinewood Road in Iver Heath.

254

Bob Monkhouse was cast as the lead in Carry On Sergeant because Anglo-Amalgamated asked for him.

255

Jimmy Logan appears in two Carry On films: Carry On Abroad, and Carry on Girls.

256

The exterior scenes for Carry On Cowboy were filed at at Chobham Common, Chobham, Woking, Surrey; Black Park Road, Wexham, Buckinghamshire and Esher Common, Esher, Surrey.

257

Kenneth Williams received £800 for his James Bailey in Carry On Sergeant.

258

One main aspect of the Carry Ons was making fun of British institutions and traditions such as the National Health Service, British Empire, army, monarchy, police, camping, holidays, schools and trade unions.

259

The Carry On films mostly received poor reviews from film critics, but were popular with cinemagoers when released.

260

Kenneth Connor appears in seventeen Carry On films:

Carry On Sergeant, Carry On Nurse, Carry On Teacher, Carry On Constable, Carry On Regardless, Carry On Cruising, Carry On Cabby, Carry On Cleo, Carry On Up the Jungle, Carry On Henry, Carry On Matron, Carry On Abroad, Carry On Girls, Carry On Dick, Carry On Behind, Carry On England and Carry On Emmanuelle.

He also appears in the Carry On Laughing and Carry On London stage productions, the 1970, 1972. and 1973 television Christmas specials, and the Carry On Laughing television series.

261

Carry On Nurse premiered in London at the Carlton Cinema on the 5th March 1959. It was released nationwide in Britain on the 23rd March 1959.

262

The Carry On films are:

Carry On Sergeant (1958)
Carry On Nurse (1959)
Carry On Teacher (1959)
Carry On Constable (1960)
Carry On Regardless (1961)
Carry On Cruising (1962)
Carry On Cabby (1963)
Carry On Jack (1964)
Carry On Spying (1964)

Carry On Cleo (1964)
Carry On Cowboy (1965)
Carry On Screaming! (1966)
Don't Lose Your Head (1967)
Follow That Camel (1967)
Carry On Doctor (1967)
Carry On Up the Khyber (1968)
Carry On Camping (1969)
Carry On Again Doctor (1969)
Carry On Up the Jungle (1970)
Carry On Loving (1970)
Carry On Henry (1971)
Carry On at Your Convenience (1971)
Carry On Matron (1972)
Carry On Abroad (1972)
Carry On Girls (1973)
Carry On Dick (1974)
Carry On Behind (1975)
Carry On England (1976)
That's Carry On! (1977)
Carry On Emmannuelle (1978)
Carry On Columbus (1992)

263

Plans were made in 2019 to film three new Carry On films simultaneously. Brian Baker won a legal battle with British television company ITV for the films. Filming was postponed after the pandemic in 2020. Baker planned to use old footage of Barbara Windsor and remake Carry On Sergeant.

The films were not made and Carry On Films Ltd, Bakers company, has been dissolved.

264

Amanda Barrie could not drive. So when she was driving her taxi in Carry On Cabby her car was towed by another car.

265

The Carry On producers announced that Carry On England would feature Kenneth Williams, Penelope Keith, Carol Hawkins, James Bolam, Ian Lavender, Susan Penhaligon and Adrienne Posta. None of these actors appeared in Carry On England.

266

On the 19th and 20th July 2010 a two hour Carry On documentary was broadcast on BBC Radio 2 in 2 parts. Titled Carry On Forever!, it was presented by Leslie Phillips.

267

The Carry On series was first released as a DVD box-set by ITV Studios Home Entertainment on 1st September 2008.

268

Carry On Spying was going to be filmed in colour. But the producers were offered some cheap monochrome film, so decided to use that.

269

The role of the police inspector in Carry On Girls was initially given to Bill Maynard. But, Maynard could not be in the Carry On as he had a television job. The role went to David Lodge.

270

Hattie Jacques was to have had a big part in Carry On Regardless, But illness meant she only had a cameo.

271

Carry On producer Peter Rogers was a custodian of the series as well as making a lot of money from the series. His nickname was Mr Carry On.

272

The Nursing Home in Carry On Again Doctor is in Iver Grove, Wood Lane, Iver Heath, Buckinghamshire.

273

In The Movies It Doesn't Hurt (1975), a short film on laboratory safety for schools, is hosted by Bernard Bresslaw and features several clips from the Carry On films.

274

Kenneth Cope appears in two Carry On films: Carry On At Your Convenience and Carry On Matron.

275

After Carry On Nurse, writer Norman Hudis researched a police themed film at Slough police station. He thought the police station setting would be a bit dull for a Carry On, so it was decided to have Carry On Teacher as the next film. After Teacher, Hudis returned to his police idea and wrote Carry On

Constable.

276

In Carry On Abroad, the Elsbels Airport is the security block at Pinewood Studios.

277

Sidney James was not available for Carry On Behind as he was In Australia performing in the play The Mating Season.

278

There were stage shows based on the Carry Ons featuring many of the Carry On film cast members.

Carry On London was staged between October 1973 and March 1975 at the Victoria Palace Theatre in London. This was a successful production written by Talbot Rothwell and Dave Freeman. Kenneth Williams and Joan Sims turned down the offer to appear. The cast included Sid James, Barbara Windsor, Peter Butterworth, Kenneth Connor, Jack Douglas and Bernard Bresslaw.

Carry On Laughing: The Slimming Factory was staged at the Royal Opera House in Scarborough in the summer of 1976 with Carry On regulars Peter Butterworth, Kenneth Connor and Jack Douglas. It was written by Sam Cree.

In 1992 Bernard Bresslaw and Barbara Windsor appeared on stage in the Barry Cryer & Dick Vosbugh penned Wot A Carry On In Blackpool.

279

On their way to the camping shop in Carry On Camping, Sid and Bernie drive down Maidenhead High Street.

280

The ballroom sequence in Carry On Don't Lose Your Head was filmed at Clandon Park, West Clandon, Surrey. Sadly, there was fire at the house in 2015 which caused lots of damage to the building and destroyed furniture and paintings.

281

Carry On Cabby is more realistic than the previous Carry Ons. It deals with the strain on the relationship between Charlie and Peggy due to work and running a business.

282

Professor Tinkle (Frankie Howerd) gives his lecture in Carry On Up The Jungle in Maidenhead Library. The library was demolished in 1974, with a new library being built.

283

Esma Cannon appears in four Carry On films: Carry On Constable, Carry On Regardless, Carry On Cruising and Carry On Cabby.

284

Nicholas Parsons appeared in Carry On Regardless. But he never worked on another Carry On as director Gerald Thomas told Parsons's agent that he was "too fussy for asking for a second take" and would not be asked back.

285

The film poster for Carry On Spying is based on the original poster art from the James Bond film From Russia With Love.

286

Carry On Cruising's premiere was held onboard a cruise ship in Southampton, England.

287

Some alternate titles for Carry On Camping were:

"Girls Camping" (Netherlands), "Holidays, Lets Go" (Poland), "Control Yourself, Hiker" (Spain), "The Trouble With Camping" (Portugal) and "I Want a Nudist Girlfriend" (South America).

288

The British War Office assisted in the making of Carry On Sergeant. Filming took place at Stoughton Barracks - home of the Queen's Royal Regiment (West Surrey). The War Office also allowed a Sergeant Major to work on the film.

289

In Carry On At Your Convenience, there is a coach trip back from Brighton where the gang stop at numerous pubs. The reflection on the side of the coach shows them getting on and off the coach at the same location.

290

Arthur Upmore's house in Carry On Behind is in Pinewood Close.

291

Kenneth Williams turned down the role of the Doctor in Carry On Screaming! at first as he did not want to play an older person. His character was changed from being Valeria's father to her brother.

292

In The Smiths song Some Girls Are Bigger Than Others, the line "As Anthony said to Cleopatra, as he opened a crate of ale, oh, I say" references Carry On Cleo.

293

Percival Snooper's (Kenneth Williams) house in Carry On Loving is on Adelaide Square, Windsor.

294

Haven Hospital in Carry On Nurse is Heatherden Hall at Pinewood Studios.

295

Carry On Matron finished filming in November 1971. It was released in May of the next year, 1972.

296

Woody Allen was considered for the role of Sergeant Nocker in Carry On Follow That Camel.

297

Yutte Stensgaard had a role in Carry On Loving, but her scene was cut from the final film.

298

For Carry On Cabby, Jim Dale worked 5 days. He was paid £160.

299

The famous scene in Carry On Camping where Barbara Windsor's bra flew off needed several takes because of technical problems.

300

Bill Pertwee (who plays ARP Warden Hodges in Dad's Army) played the manager of The Whippit Inn bar in Carry On Up Your Convenience. Unfortunately his scenes were deleted.

301

Carry On Dick was planned for 1974. But, it was not sure if Talbot Rothwell would write another Carry On film. The producers asked Lawrie Wyman and George Evans to write the script. Rothwell did return to write the script, and kept Wyman and Evans's plot.

302

Maudlin Street School in Carry On Teacher is Drayton Secondary School in West Ealing, London.

303

Gerald Thomas directed all the Carry On films.

304

Carry On Matron was completed filming six and a half days ahead of schedule.

305

Roy Castle appears in one Carry On film: Carry On Up The Khyber.

306

Sid James recalled a time when he was on holiday in Honolulu and thought he may have problems with the custom's officer:

"So he looks at my passport, then he looks down at me from his 18ft and I turned to my wife and said, 'Here we go.' However, he shouts in a voice that blows the place apart, 'CAAARRY OOOONNN!'.And he took [my wife] and I straight through customs. Straight through the lot."

307

Carry On Nurse was popular in the US. It played at some cinemas for three years

308

During filming of Carry On Girls on Brighton's West Pier, the crew were warned that the pier was in a dangerous condition and not to to too far along it. The pier has been derelict since 1975 (Carry On Girls was filmed in 1973) and has now mostly collapsed into the sea.

309

The Nurses accommodation building in Carry On Doctor is at Westbourne Street, London. The building is opposite Hyde Park.

310

Joan Sims was second, behind Kenneth Williams, in the number of Carry On appearances.

311

Barbara Windsor could not ride a motorbike, so her motorbike riding scenes in Carry On Girls were done by a stuntman

312

The 1970 Carry On Christmas television special, Carry On Again Christmas, was made in black and white. This is because technicians at ITV were on strike and refusing to use colour television equipment.

313

South Africa banned Carry On Dick because of Sid James's role as a crooked vicar.

314

Dave Freeman wrote two Carry On film scripts - Carry On Behind and Carry On Columbus.

He also wrote the Carry On Again Christmas special in 1970, co-wrote the 1972 Carry On Christmas special with Talbot Rothwell, wrote several episodes of the Carry On Laughing television series, and co-wrote the Carry On London stage show (with Talbot Rothwell).

Freeman provided a wonderful script for Carry On Behind. But his Carry On Columbus script was less successful. He had only a few weeks to write the script, and the completed film was a bit of a mess.

Freeman wrote numerous comedy scripts from the earliest days of British television in the 1950s. He wrote for comedians such as Arthur Askey, Tommy Cooper, Frankie Howerd and Spike Milligan

315

In the scene in Carry On Cleo where British slaves escape out of a window, one man can be seen wearing red underpants.

316

For Carry On Behind, Caravans International provided caravans and sponsored the film. The famous caravan and motorhome company went out of business in 1982.

317

When Sergeant Bung drives his car in Carry On Screaming,

the Johnny Todd song is played; this is theme to the BBC television police drama Z Cars.

318

Carry On England has some stock footage of British and German aircraft from the film The Battle of Britain (1969).

319

When the Carry On producers made a deal with Rank to distribute the films, Rank did not want the Carry On prefix to be used as it was associated with previous distributor Anglo Amalgamated.

320

Guy Fawkes (Bill Maynard) appears in Carry On Henry. But, Guy Fawkes was born 23 years after Henry VIII died.

321

While filming Carry On Doctor, Barbara Windsor was appearing on stage in the evening in The Beggars Opera at the Connaught Theatre in Worthing.

322

Ted Ray was going to play Sergeant Wilkins in Carry On Constable, after appearing in the previous Carry On, Carry On Teacher. But, Ray was contracted to another film company, ABC. They threatened to stop distribution of Carry On Constable if Ray appeared, so he was not able to star in the film. He was replaced by Sid James for his first Carry On film.

323

Producer Peter Rogers kept costs low by insisting that the films not have a single star - apart from a few occasions when he hired a big foreign name for a bigger fee.

324

The Carry On films began in 1958 which was the year the last Ealing comedy was released.

325

The scenes between Joan Sims and Frankie Howerd in the hospital in Carry On Doctor were shot separately with the two actors and edited together. Joans Sims could not do the scenes with Howerd as she kept laughing.

326

After Carry On Spying, there were five consecutive historical Carry Ons before Carry On Doctor returned to a contemporary setting.

327

David Essex had a role in Carry On Henry as a young man at a Speaker's Corner meeting, but his scene was cut.

328

Carry On scriptwriter Norman Hudis said he would have loved to have written a Carry On based in the newspaper world in Fleet Street in London.

329

Eric Rogers took over from Bruce Montgomery as Carry On composer from Carry On Cabby. Rogers added musical jokes to the scores.

330

When Carry On Sergeant was released it was not intended to have a series of similar films called Carry On.

331

In Carry On Matron, Sir Bernard Cutting (Kenneth Williams) reads a medical book titles Metamorphosis - A Study of the Sex change in Man. The author of the book is Professor Axel Grease.

332

Anglo-Amalgamated Productions was a British film company which produced and distributed films from 1945 to the late 1960s. It made low budget films and distributed numerous famous American low budget cult films in Britain.

From 1958 to 1966 Anglo-Amalgamated distributed the first twelve Carry On films.

Carry On Sergeant (1958)
Carry On Nurse (1959)
Carry On Teacher (1959)
Carry On Constable (1960)
Carry On Regardless (1961)
Carry On Cruising (1962)
Carry On Cabby (1963)

Carry On Jack (1964)
Carry On Spying (1964)
Carry On Cleo (1964)
Carry On Cowboy (1965)
Carry On Screaming! (1966)

333

In 1989, Harry Enfield made a mock documentary about the life of a fictional actor Norbert Smith. It was shown on Channel 4, and Enfield played Smith.

In the documentary it has a three minute fictional clip of Norbert appearing in a Carry On called Carry On Banging. The film is set in the early 80s and is about the Greenham Common military base and peace protesters outside. Jack Douglas, Kenneth Connor and Barbara Windsor appear.

334

Carry On Follow That Camel (1967) had a budget of £288366. This is about at £4,460,000 today.

335

Barbara Windsor said her favourite Carry On film is Carry On Henry.

336

Peter Butterworth appears in sixteen Carry On films:

Carry On Cowboy, Carry On Screaming, Carry On Don't Lose Your Head, Carry On Follow That Camel, Carry On Doctor, Carry On Up the Khyber, Carry On Camping, Carry On Again

Doctor, Carry On Loving, Carry On Henry, Carry On Abroad, Carry On Girls, Carry On Dick, Carry On Behind, Carry On England and Carry On Emmanuelle.

Butterworth also starred in three of the Carry On Christmas specials - 1969, 1972, 1973; the Carry On Laughing television series and the Carry On London and Carry On Laughing stage shows.

337

The Rank Organisation distributed the Carry On films from from 1967 to 1978.

338

Carry On Camping was filmed in rather cold conditions in the spring. Famously, the mud was sprayed with green paint to look like grass.

339

There were four Carry On Christmas television specials, made by ITV.

The first special, Carry On Christmas, was broadcast in 1969 (written by Talbot Rothwell) with a bumper cast including Sid James, Frankie Howerd, Barbara Windsor, Bernard Bresslaw, Peter Butterworth, Hattie Jacques, Charles Hawtrey and Terry Scott. Frankie Howerd appears as the special was filmed just after Carry On Up the Jungle finished filming (which Howerd appears in). This has A Christmas Carol theme with Sid James as Scrooge.

Carry On Again Christmas was shown in 1970. It was filmed in black and white (unlike the other three specials) because of a colour film technicians strike and written by Dave Freeman and Sid Colin. This special stars Sid James, Terry Scott, Charles Hawtrey, Bernard Bresslaw, Kenneth Connor and Barbara Windsor.

The next special was Carry On Christmas (or Carry On Stuffing) shown in 1972. This was written by Talbot Rothewell and Dave Freeman. Sid James was absent, and the special stars Joan Sims, Kenneth Connor, Peter Butterworth, Barbara Windsor, Hattie Jacques and Jack Douglas. This special has an 18th Century banquet setting.

The last Carry On Christmas special was shown in Christmas 1973. Written by Talbot Rothwell, it features Sid James, Barbara Windsor, Peter Butterworth, Kenneth Connor, Bernard Bresslaw, Joan Sims and Jack Douglas. This one has Sid James as a department store Father Christmas and a selection of historical set sketches.

340

Frank Forsyth appears in eight Carry On films: Carry On Again Doctor, Carry On Sergeant, Carry On Nurse, Carry On Constable, Carry On Cabby, Carry On Jack, Carry On Carry On Spying, and Screaming.

341

Many of the cast members in Carry On Camping had character names similar to their real names. For example, Sidney James played Sid Boggle, Charles Hawtrey plays Charlie Muggins, Barbara Windsor plays Babs, Joan Sims is Joan Fussey, Bernard Bresslaw plays Bernie Lugg and Kenneth Williams is Doctor Kenneth Soaper.

342

For Carry On Cruising, Kenneth Connor was paid £4,500, Sidney James £4,000 and Kenneth Williams £5,000.

343

The University of Kidburn in Carry On Behind is Maidenhead Town Hall.

344

Kenneth Connor appeared in Carry On Cleo in 1964, and missed eight Carry On films before returning in 1970 for Carry On Up The Jungle. He unable to work on the Carry Ons because he was working on other projects such as in the theatre.

345

The first Carry On film Carry On Sergeant originated in 1955. Producer Sydney Box asked R.F. Delderfield to write a screenplay about National Service in Britain.

In 1957 Delderfield resurrected the idea with a film similar in tone to the 1944 drama The Way Ahead, which depicted the training of conscripts of the British army. In 1957 it was recommended by the British government that National Service should end. Sydney Box decided a comedy similar to Private's Progress (1956) and the television sitcom The Army Game would be successful. Box asked his brother in law Peter Rogers to make a film which became Carry On Sergeant.

346

Charles Hawtrey demanded top billing for the 1972 Carry On Christmas television special, Carry On Stuffing. This was because Sid James and Terry Scott were absent. Producer Peter Rogers gave top billing to Hattie Jacques, so Hawtrey pulled out of the special at short notice.

347

Cor Blimey! 2000 television adaption by Terry Johnson of his 1998 stage play Cleo, Camping, Emmanuelle and Dick! The television version received good reviews.

It's about the relationship between Sid James and Barbara Windsor. Sid James is played by Geoffrey Hutchings, Barbara Windsor by Samantha Spiro and Kenneth Williams is played by Adam Godley.

This television adaption features more locations and other Carry On actors and characters than the stage play.

348

Carry On Nurse was written by Norman Hudis. It was based on the play Ring for Catty written Patrick Cargill and Jack Beale

349

Angela Douglas appears in four Carry On films:

Carry On Cowboy, Carry on Screaming, Carry on Follow That Camel and Carry On Up The Khyber.

350

Bob Monkhouse turned down the role of Ted York in Carry On Nurse. The role was played by Terence Longdon.

351

James Beck - Private Walker in Dad's Army - and Yutte Stensgaard had a cameo as husband and wife in Carry On Loving but it was cut.

352

British newspaper The Times did not have a positive review of Carry On Constable:

"Little to recommend it. Good ideas are few, and there is material here for little more than a modest series of television sketches farcically involving the police"

353

Some other titles for Carry On Up the Khyber are:

"Carry On Gunga Din" (Denmark), "Carry On Khyber Strait" (Hungary) and "Argument in the Khyber" (Poland).

354

A double ententre is a phrase which has two meanings: a phrase can be innocent but also have a sexual meaning. The Carry On films are famous for their double ententres and they are a key part of the humour.

355

Angela Douglas (1940-) appears in four Carry On films. Carry On Cowboy (1965), Carry On Screaming! (1966), Carry On Follow That Camel (1967) and Carry On Up The Khyber (1968).

356

Private detective James Bedsop (Charles Hawtrey) follows Sid Bliss (Sid James) up Windsor High Street.

357

Steptoe and son actor Wilfred Brambell appears in Carry On Again Doctor in a small no speaking role. The theme from Steptoe and Son plays when he is on screen

358

Carry On Behind (1975) was Ian Lavender's only Carry On.

359

Carry On Sergeant was the third most successful movie at the British box office in 1958.

360

Carry On Columbus was filmed between 21st April – 27th May 1992, so the 27th May was the last filming date for a Carry On.

361

The role of the Private Easy in Carry On England was played by Diane Langdon. It was written for Barbara Windsor. She could not appear in the film as she was in Shakespeare play Twelfth Night running at the Chichester Festival Theatre.

362

In Carry On Sergeant, the National Service recruits should be around 20 years old. But they were played by older actors such as Charles Hawtrey, who was over 40 when the film was made.

363

Jack Douglas received a crate of champagne as part of his payment for Carry On Matron.

364

Carry On Nurse nurse grossed $843,000 at the British box office.

365

When production started on Carry On Sergeant, it was going to be a drama film.

366

Barbara Windsor appears in ten Carry On Films: Carry On Spying, Carry On Doctor, Carry On Camping, Carry On Again Doctor, Carry On Henry, Carry On Matron, Carry On Abroad, Carry On Girls, Carry On Dick, That's Carry On!.

She appeared in all four of the Christmas television specials. Also appeared in the Carry On Laughing television series, the 1973 Carry On London stage production, and with Jack

Douglas in the 1992 What A Carry On stage production.

367

In Carry On Girls, Mayor Frederick Bumble has his trousers ripped off at Windsor Fire Station.

368

Director Gerald Thomas tried to a Carry On film quickly and not have too many takes. At the end of film party for Carry On Matron Thomas announced that the film ended shooting six and a half days ahead of schedule. Kenneth Williams noted in his diary: "he said it was a record for him. I should think it was a record for the industry."

369

The Barrier/Guard Room in Carry On England is in Pinewood Studios.

370

Val Guest was asked to direct the first Carry On, Carry On Sergeant.

371

StudioCanal has released several early Carry Ons on Blu-ray. Australian company Via Vision have released the films up to Carry On Screaming in three box sets.

372

The British censors had problems with the name Sarah

Allcock (played by Joan Sims) in Carry On Teacher. They did not like the way cock was announced clearly by other characters. But the name was able to be used.

373

The brothel keeper in Carry On Abroad is played by Olga Lowe. Lowe worked with Sid James early in his career in Britain. Sadly, she was on stage with James when he died on stage in Sunderland.

374

Seventeen year old Larry Dann appears in Carry On Teacher (as one of the boys. He came back to the series for three of the later entries Carry on Behind, Carry on England and Carry on Emmannuelle with larger roles.

375

Producer Peter Rogers said the title of the film was the star, but three actors had their name in special billing in the credits: Bob Monkhouse in Carry on Sergeant (1958), Ted Ray in Carry On Teacher and Phil Silvers in Carry on Follow That Camel (1967).

376

Dandy Nichols appears in one Carry On film: Carry On Doctor (1967).

377

Sid James built his own house near Pinewood studios. This meant he was able to go home for lunch when filming many of the Carry Ons.

378

Carry on Copper was considered for the title of Carry on Constable.

379

Talbot Rothwell was not available to write the script for Carry On Behind. Dave Freeman wrote the script.

380

Carry On Emmannuelle was given a AA certificate in Britain, excluding under 14 year olds. This was due to the sexual nature of the film.

381

Scriptwriter Norman Hudis did not like the drunken operation scene in Carry On Nurse. He said it was "an absurd scene that didn't work".

382

While filming Carry On Nurse, Kenneth Williams kept falling asleep. This was sue to acting in bed underneath hot studio lights. Director Gerald Thomas would wake him up, only for Kenny to complain that he was not sleeping. One time when Williams feel asleep, Thomas put a sign around his neck and took a photo. The next time Kenny fell asleep, he was shown the photo!

383

Carry On Up The Khyber is a spoof of films and television series, and stories by authors such as Rudyard Kipling about the British Raj - British rule in India.

384

Michael Nightingale appeared in thirteen Carry Ons, and made more Carry On appearances than any other member of the supporting cast. Four were uncredited appearances: Carry On Regardless, Don't Lose Your Head, Follow That Camel, and Carry On Girls). His credited roleswere in Carry On Cabby, Carry On Jack, Carry On Cleo, Carry On Cowboy, Carry On Camping, Carry On Matron, Carry On Dick, Carry On England, and Carry On Emmanuelle.

He also appeared in two episodes of the Carry On Laughing TV series.

385

Kenneth Connor's son Jeremy plays his character Bernie's son in Carry On Nurse. Jeremy only said his lines when the director Gerald Thomas promised him sweets.

386

In Carry On Abroad Jimmy Logan falls into some wet cement. In reality the cement was grey coloured porridge.

387

Carry On Up the Jungle was going to be called Carry On Tarzan. "Tarzan" was owned by the estate of Edgar Rice

Burroughs who created the character and it did not let the Carry On producers use the character name.

388

Carry On Screaming! is the longest Carry On film at 98 minutes.

389

Kenneth Connor never watched his own performances; but he watched Carry On Nurse as his son Jeremy was in it.

390

Frankie Howerd and Kenneth Connor had an argument in a stage show before the filming of Carry On Up The Jungle. The producers had to ensure they got on during filming of the Carry On film.

391

In Carry On Nurse, the Colonel (Wilfred Hyde White) stick an L plate on Stella's (Joan Sims) back; it disappears in the next shot.

392

Norman Hudis admitted he was struggling to write the Carry Ons, starting with Carry On Regardless. The next film, Carry On Cruising, was his last. Later his successor as scriptwriter Talbot Rothwell suffered from nervous exhaustion writing his last Carry On, Carry On Dick.

393

The title Carry On Holiday was considered for Carry On Cruising.

394

Upper Dencher church in Carry On Dick has a First World War memorial outside.

395

Billy Cornelius appears in eight Carry Ons: Carry On Screaming, Carry On Again Doctor, Carry On Henry, Carry On Dick, Carry On Cowboy, Carry On Girls and Carry On Don't Lose Your Head.

He also appeared in the 1970 Carry On Stuffing Christmas TV special, and three episodes on the Carry On Laughing TV series.

396

Sid James was appearing in the pantomime Babes in the Wood at the London Palladium until June 1966. He was not available for Carry On Screaming! which was filmed in January and February 1966. Harry H. Corbett replaced James.

397

Edward Scaife was the cinematographer for Carry On Constable. He was unavailable for the next film Carry On Regardless as he a had a job in Turkey. Producer Peter Rogers only had a few days to find a replacement. He asked Alan Hume, the director of photography, to do the role. Hume did so, and went to become the regular Carry On cinematographer for fourteen films.

398

In the BBC television sitcom, Taxi! Sid James plays London cabby Sid Stone - a similar character to the one he plays in Cabby On Cabby. Taxi! ran from 1963-64.

399

At some cinemas showing Carry On Screaming, you could but Kreepy Kwivers rubberised monster toys, for the price of 12/6; this is 12 shillings and 6 pence. About £5 in 2024 prices.

400

Harry Secombe was considered for the part of Henry VIII in Carry On Henry. Originally it was planned for Henry to sing madrigals, and Secombe was a tenor.

401

Patsy Rowlands said that when several guests visited the set of Carry On Matron, Kenneth Williams mooned at them.

402

The voice of Doctor Crow in Carry On Spying is provided by John Bluthal. Bluthal plays Corporal Clotski in Carry On Follow That Camel.

403

Lance Percival said there were technical problems with the

exploding chef scene in Carry On Cruising:

"They were trying to get the cake to blow up in my face. It was done with a pressure pump underneath with the cake mixture sitting on top of an air pipe. When they pressed a button, the mixture was to shoot all over my face. However, every time I leaned over to 'smell the aroma' just before it exploded, I blinked as it actually shot up i.e. I knew it was coming! Therefore, it took nine takes to get a scene that lasts ten seconds - unheard of in a Carry On".

404

Both the BBC and ITV in the UK had their own popular television shows made up of clips from the Carry On films in the 1980s.

Thames Television produced Carry On Laughing (reusing the title of the 1970's original television series). 12 episodes were made between 1981-83.

BBC produced What A Carry On. 13 episodes were made and were first broadcast between 1984-87.

Laugh with the Carry Ons was compiled in 1993 and produced by ITV.

These clip programmes were produced by Peter Rogers, and edited by Rogers and Gerald Thomas.

Many of the surviving Carry On actors were annoyed that they did not receive repeat fee royalties from these clip shows.

405

Fenella Fielding appears in two Carry On films: Carry On Regardless and Carry On Screaming!.

406

W.C Boggs & Son's toilet factory in Carry On At Your Convenience is the timber yard in Pinewood Studios.

407

Carry On Sergeant had preview screenings for cinema owners on the 1st August 1958, and screenings in certain regions such as Birmingham before being released nationally on the 20th September.

408

Valerie Leon made her Carry On debut in Carry On Up the Khyber. She had an uncredited role as a Hospitality girl.

409

Some of Carry On Cruising titles included:

"Girls at Sea" (Denmark), "Watch Out for the Cabins" (South America), "Mediterranean Cruise" (Greece), and "The Ships Cook is Seasick" (Germany).

410

A Carry On London film was in production in the early 2000s; near the end of the abandoned project, the name of the film was changed to Carry On Bananas.

411

Carry On Sergeant was Bernard Kay's first film.

412

Eric Barker had an idea for a Carry On about a European coach tour. Producer Peter Rogers though the idea would work better with a Mediterranean cruise and asked Barker to write a 40 page treatment. The treatment became Carry On Cruising.

413

That Mitchell and Webb Look is a BBC sketch show that ran from 2006 to 2010; it stars David Mitchell and Robert Webb. One sketch spoofing the Carry Ons in the show has a Bawdy 1970s Hospital, where everyone uses double ententres; one Doctor does not understand the concept and keeps using rude phrases instead of double ententres and is reprimanded.

414

Jim Dale appears in eleven Carry On films:

Carry On Cabby, Carry On Jack, Carry On Spying, Carry On Cleo, Carry On Cowboy, Carry On Screaming, Carry On Don't Lose Your Head, Carry On Doctor, Carry On Follow That Camel, Carry On Again Doctor and Carry On Columbus.

415

Carry On Cowboy was inspired by comedy western such as The Paleface (1948) starring Bob Hope and The Sheriff of Fractured Jaw (1958) with Kenneth More. The Sheriff of

Fractured Jaw depicted an Englishman in the wild west, and both these comedies had buffonish heroes who were thought to be crack shots, but in reality female characters were the crack shots.

416

In Carry On Henry, Sid James wore the same costume worn by Richard Burton playing another Henry VIII in the film Anne of the Thousand Days.

417

After watching Carry On Up the Khyber, an Indian living in England thanked Bernard Bresslaw for showing India in the film: Bresslaw did not reveal the film was shot in Wales.

418

The Police Station in Carry On Dick is the servants quarters at Stoke Poges Manor House, Stoke Poges, Buckinghamshire.

419

In 2016 Jonathan Sothcott of Hereford Films announced that the company would make a series of new Carry On films. Titles would include Carry On Campus and Carry On Doctors. In 2017 Sothcott said he had no plans to make any Carry Ons.

420

Fenella Fielding turned down a role in Carry On Cabby. She thought the film concentrated on her cleavage too much!

421

Carry On at Your Convenience did not make much money in the British cinemas. For the next film it was decided to make Carry On Matron as medical Carry Ons were popular.

422

Carry On Jack is the first Carry On film in which Kenneth Connor does not appear.

423

Carry On Emmannuelle release on home video was delayed after arguments over its certificate.

424

Kenneth Cope was considered for the role of Midshipman Albert Poop Decker in Carry On Cruising. The role went to Bernard Cribbins.

425

The Carry On films were filmed in about six weeks and then in the cinema a few months later. This meant that topical jokes and content could be included.

426

Director Gerald Thomas enjoyed Carry On Jack for its "pantomime qualities".

427

During the filming of the conveyor belt scene in Carry On Spying, Charles Hawtrey fainted. It was thought it was due to fright, but he was drunk.

A nurse asked Hawtrey if anyone had given him some brandy. "That's the last thing he needs, dear." Kenneth Williams said!

428

Marianne Stone appears in nine Carry On films: Carry On Nurse, Carry On Constable, Carry On Jack, Carry On Screaming!, Carry On Don't Lose Your Head, Carry On Doctor, Carry On at Your Convenience, Carry On Girls, Carry On Dick and Carry On Behind.

429

Kenneth Williams uses his catchphrase "stop messing about!" for the first time in a Carry On film in Carry On Spying.

430

The interior of the Reverend Flashers house in Carry On Dick is in Stoke Poges Manor House, Stoke Poges, Buckinghamshire.

431

Alan Hume was the cinematographer for Carry On Spying. He was the cinematographer for three James Bond films: For Your Eyes Only (1981), Octopussy (1983) and A View to a Kill (1985).

432

Eric Barker appears in Carry On Sergeant, Carry On Constable and Carry On Spying before appearing in Carry On Emmannuelle.

433

The Parade Ground in Carry On Sergeant was the Queens Barracks in Guildford. The site is now a housing development.

434

The music playing as the agents enter the automation area in Carry On Spying is used in the 1983 animated television series Dungeons and Dragons.

435

On 7 October 2013 the Carry On DVD Box set collection was re-released with smaller packaging.

436

The Old Cock Inn in Carry On Dick is the Jolly Woodman Pub in Littleworth Common, Buckinghamshire.

437

Esme Crowfoot's (Joan Sims) flat in Carry On Loving is in Atherton Court in Eton, Berkshire.

438

The spoof voice over narrator for Carry On Cleo was E.V.H.

Emmett who voiced British newsreels for Gaumont between the 1930s-50s.

439

An Australian set film, Carry On Down Under, was planned for the early 1980s. Kenneth Williams and Hattie Jacques signed up. Unfortunately the project was abandoned after Hattie's death in 1980.

440

Jim Dale did his own stunts for the scene in Carry On Again Doctor where Dr Nookey is drunk. He injured himself and suffered back problems for years afterwards.

441

In Carry On Girls, Bernard Bresslaw has the same name used by Terry Scott in Carry On Camping - Peter Potter.

442

For Carry On Cowboy, Kenneth Williams based on voice on American film producer Hal Roach.

443

Carry On Spying was one of the first James Bond parody films. Another early James Bond parody as Hot Enough For June, directed by Gerald Thomas's brother Ralph, and produced Peter Rogers's wife Betty E. Box.

444

Carry On Cowboy was the first Carry On film for Peter Butterworth and Bernard Bresslaw.

445

Sid James is the top billed star for Carry On Again Doctor. But, he first appears after 37 minutes.

446

The full name of the trade union NUCIE in Carry On At Your Convenience is the National Union of Chinaware Industrial Employees.

447

The part of Private Alice Easy in Carry On England was written for Barbara Windsor. In the end the role went to Diane Langton, who is rather like Windsor.

448

Carry On Emmannuelle (1978) (£320000) had a bigger budget than Carry On Columbus (1992) (£2500000).

449

The cinema in Carry On At Your Convenience was the Odeon cinema on Uxbridge High Street. The cinema was demolished in 1984.

450

In Carry On Screaming, Fenella Fielding only had one red dress for her character; she wore it for five weeks of filming.

451

In Carry On Behind, the signs in Fred Ramsden's butcher's shop say the shop is closing for the Easter holiday.

452

Sid James was 46 years old when he made his first Carry On film, Carry On Constable, in 1960.

453

Charles Hawtrey was a late casting for Carry On Screaming!, replacing Sydney Bromley who was going to play Dan Dann. Hawtrey was requested by the film's American distributors.

454

Carry On Screaming has a similar plot to the Vincent Price horror film House of Wax (1953), which has women abducted and encased in wax.

455

One of the reasons Bob Monkhouse turned down a role in Carry On Nurse is that he thought the fee was too low.

456

In Carry On Abroad it was originally planned for Charles

Hawtrey to play a solicitor called Charles Makepeace.

457

One idea for Carry On Screaming! was to cast Vincent Price to appeal to American audiences. The role of Dr Watt was written for him; the role was played by Kenneth Williams.

458

Barbara Windsor turned down the role of Queen Isabella in Carry On Columbus.

459

Liz Fraser said Carry On Regardless was her favourite of the four Carry Ons she appeared in.

460

Charles Hawtrey filmed all his scenes as Dan Dann in Carry On Screaming! in one day.

461

Carry On Cabby is an interesting Carry On in that it has quite a serious, dramatic plotline which depicts a troubled marriage.

462

Carry On England had a AA rating on release in Britain. This meant the film was for over 14's only. The rating was due to topless nudity and the someone saying Fokker (a German aircraft) which sounded like a rude word! The scenes were cut and the film was re-released with an A rating - the same as the previous Carry Ons.

463

During the filming of Carry On Don't Lose Your Head, Sid James was appearing in the evening at the Pier Theatre in Bournemouth in Wedding Fever.

464

ITV include one censored line when showing Carry On Don't Lose Your Head after 9 pm. This is the line where Desiree Dubarry (Joan Sims) says to Duc de Pommfrit (Charles Hawtrey) says "my cousin, the count" in away in which count sounds like a rather rude swear word. In 2016 ITV actually showed the version of the film with this line in it at 7 am.

465

Kenneth Connor's contract for Carry On Cleo included a clause that stated he would still be allowed to work on his very successful West End stage show A Funny Thing Happened On The Way To The Forum with Frankie Howerd.

466

Carry On Don't Lose Your Head was the first Carry On to star a non-British actor: Dany Robin was French.

467

Kenneth Williams said to Jim Dale and Peter Butterworth on the set of Carry On Follow That Camel that the other person did not like them. Dale and Butterworth had most of their scenes together and this caused problems at the start of filming as they were not talking. Eventually, they found out that Kenny had played a trick on them.

468

Carry On Nurse had the biggest British cinema audience of any Carry On: 10.4 million people saw it.

469

Carry On Sergeant is the shortest Carry On film at 84 minutes.

470

For Carry On Regardless, director Gerald Thomas filmed a scene as a shop assistant who sells Sam some cigarettes, but it was cut from the final scene.

471

Carry On producer Peter Roger's and director Gerald Thomas were both millionaires from the Carry On series. Both had a percentage of the takings, unlike the cast who took a flat fee from each film. Rogers said he offered the actors a percentage of the takings, but they turned it down.

Leslie Phillips said when Rogers died in 2009: "Since he made all those people famous the world has changed in every conceivable way. Contracts were not sorted out in those days. People that I knew and worked with him, they all loved him in spite of all that. We did have a wonderful time in those days but we weren't paid wonderful money."

472

June Whitfield appears in four Carry On films: Carry On Nurse, Carry On Abroad, Carry On Girls and Carry On Columbus.

473

In Carry On Dick, white lines can be seen painted in the middle of the road as Kenneth Williams and Jack Douglas are riding on horseback.

474

For Carry On Doctor, On producer Peter Rogers was worried about having two big camp stars Kenneth Williams and Frankie Howerd in the same film. Rogers later said he tried to keep them apart on screen, but they have some scenes together.

475

In Carry On Follow That Camel, the World War 2 marching song Durch die grüne Heide is played on a gramophone. Carry On Follow That Camel is set in 1906.

476

Carry On Sergeant was inspired by the ITV television sitcom The Army Game (1957-1961).

477

In Carry On Nurse, a daffodil in used instead of a rectal thermometer. In Carry On Doctor, a nurse goes up to Mr Bigger (Frankie Howerd) with a daffodil; Bigger says "Oh no you don't! I saw that film!"

478

Dr Watt's house in Carry On Screaming! is Fulmer Grange which is near Pinewood Studios.

479

Pintpot (Charles Hawtrey) in Carry On Cabby learns to drive his cab on Arthur Road in Windsor.

480

Carry On producer Peter Rogers's wife Betty E. Box produced the Doctor series of films. As a result, a percentage of the takings for Carry On Doctor was given to Box for the use of he Doctor title.

481

Jacki Piper appears in four Carry On films: Carry Up The Jungle, Carry On Loving, Carry On At Your Convenience and Carry On Matron.

482

Carry On Columbus made more money in British cinemas in 1992 than two other big Hollywood Christopher Columbus films released in 1992: Christopher Columbus: The Discovery and 1492: Conquest of Paradise.

483

Some alternative titles for Carry On Follow That Camel are:

"Carry On in the Legion" (USA), "In the Desert, No Water Flows" (West Germany) and "Carry On with the Foreign Legion" (Hungary).

484

Brian Wilde appears in one Carry On: Carry On Doctor.

485

David Lodge appears in five Carry On films: Carry On Regardless, Carry On Girls, Carry On Dick, Carry On Behind, and Carry On England.

He also appeared in 7 episodes of the Carry On Laughing television series.

486

The early Carry On films had a theme of different and disorganised individuals in a British institution working together. This theme was similar to that of the Eailing comedies.

487

In Carry On Doctor, Mr Bigger's name tag by his bed is spelled Mr Biggir.

488

In Carry On Up the Khyber, Lady Ruff Diamond's line, "Oh dear! I seem to have got a little plastered," was an ad lib by Joan Sims and was used in the film.

489

The coach used in the trip to Brighton in Carry On At Your Convenience was from Denham Coaches. Denham Coaches was owned By Jack Crump, and his coach business garage was in the grounds of Pinewood. His coaches appear in several other Carry On films, and his business had lots of work moving production teams to locations.

490

At the start of each Rank Carry On, the Rank company introduction features a gongman banging a gong. In Carry On Up the Khyber, a gong is banged and the Khasi (Kenneth Williams) describes it as "rank stupidity".

491

Hattie Jacques was asked to play a lead role in Carry On Regardless. But, she was ill during filming so had a small role as a matron in a hospital.

492

The hospital in Carry On Doctor is Maidenhead Town Hall in Maidenhead, Berkshire.

493

In Carry On Cabby, the newly married couples' house is located on Pinewood Green Estate.

494

The scene where Bernard Bresslaw rides a motor bike in Carry

On At Your Convenience took many takes due to Bernard's lack of riding skills.

495

During the dinner scene in Carry On Up the Khyber, the actors did not want to eat any of the food, especially as dust and debris was falling into it. They pushed the food around and had to eat something as the scene went on. but, Director Gerald Thomas had played a joke as he had ended the scene without telling the cast.

496

In Carry On Constable, Charles Hawtrey gets out of bed and steps in his chamber pot. It rolls around on the floor and he tells it to be quiet. this line is improvised.

497

During the filming of Carry On Up the Khyber, Angela Douglas lost an earring. Because of continuity, she had to hide one ear for the rest of filming.

498

Jim Dale was offered the part of the coach driver (played by Julian Holloway in the film) in Carry On Camping, but was busy.

499

Carry On nurse was the most successful British film in the US, until Four Weddings and a Funeral became more successful in 1994.

500

Carry On at Your Convenience was a box office failure in Britain. One reason for the unpopularity of the film was thought to have been the anti-trade union theme of the film which put off working class cinemagoers.

501

Dick Van Dyke was filming Chitty Chitty Bang Bang at Pinewood at the same time as Carry On Up the Khyber. He visited the set of the Carry On.

502

Wanda Ventham appears in Carry On Up the Khyber as The Khasi's First Wife. In 2021, she appeared on BBC antique bidding television series The Bidding Room. She had a Carry On Up the Khyber poster signed by the cast. She was offered £1000 but did not sell.

503

For Carry On Cruising, cruise liner company P&O ran a competition to win an expensive cruise holiday.

504

In Carry On Regardless, Montgomery Infield-Hopping (Terence Longdon) drives on Fairfield Road in Yiewsley, Hillingdon, London.

505

In the dinner scene at the end of Carry On Up the Khyber, the ceiling collapses and dust falls on Sir Sidney Ruff-Diamond's (Sid James) shoulder. The size of the dust changes from scene to scene.

506

Carry On Cruising was filmed on a replica of a cruise ship at Pinewood Studios.

507

In Carry On Again Doctor Jim Dale performed all his own stunts. He broke his arm during the film.

508

During the filming of Carry On Camping, Betty Marsden (who played Harriet Potter) said to Dilys Laye that she would like to die with a glass of gin in her hand. Betty died in 1998 at Denville Hall, the retirement home for actors, while drinking gin at he home's bar.

509

Scriptwriter Norman Hudis did not like his script for Carry On Regardless, calling it "a mess". In particular he disliked the part where Sam Twist tries to give up smoking.

510

Location filming for Carry On Follow That Camel at Camber Sands in East Sussex had to be stopped numerous times because of snow.

511

In 1998 Terry Johnson wrote a play about the love affair between Sid James ans Barbara Windsor. It is set on the locations of the Carry Ons and called Cleo, Camping, Emmanuelle and Dick. The Carry On members portrayed in the cast of six are Sid James (Geoffrey Hutchings), Barbara Windsor (Samantha Spiro), Kenneth Williams (Adam Godley) and Imogen Hassell (Gina Bellman). The play has god reviews, and it was turned into a television play by ITV called Cor Blimey! in 2000.

512

Carry On Camping had its British premiere in Hull, Yorkshire.

513

Joan Sims had a nasty accident during filming for Carry On Nurse. In the scene where Nurse Dawson has an accident with a trolley and falls over, she got a gash in her shin and had to be taken to hospital for stitches.

514

In Carry On Screaming, the tune Old Ned is played when Sergeant Bung rides on the horse and cart. Old Ned is the theme tune to the BBC television comedy Steptoe and Son, in which Sergeant Bung actor Harry H. Corbett stars.

515

Barbara Windsor planned to play her character in Carry On Camping with an upper class, posh English accent. But, in her first scene where she looks through the know hole in the shower, she said her lines in her usual cockney accent. As director Gerald Thomas refused to have another take, Barbara had to do the film with her usual cockney accent.

516

Carry On Cowboy ran over the planned filming schedule by a day. This was caused by bad weather at the start of filming.

517

The governor's residence in Carry On Up The Khyber was the administrative offices of Pinewood Studios.

518

In Carry On At Your Convenience, the coach party have their Brighton lunch booked at Clarges Hotel, Brighton.

519

During a love scene between Kenneth Williams and Joan Sims in Carry On up the Khyber, Kenny broke wind during the scene - which did not please Joan!

520

When Carry On producer Peter Rogers died, he left money from estate and future royalties of the Carry Ons to the Cinema and Television Benevolent Fund which helps those who work behind the scenes in film and television.

521

One proposed title for Carry On Jack was Carry On Mate.

522

The hippy dance scene in Carry On Camping took two days to film.

523

In Carry On Behind the stripper makes her entrance and the music tape is switched on; but the tape does not move.

524

Some alternative titles for Carry On Abroad are:

"What a Holiday" (Denmark), "The Shopping Spree" (Portugal), "A Completely Mad Holiday" (Germany), and "Looking for the Sun Abroad" (Belgium).

525

Sid James wrote this to producer Peter Rogers when he read the Carry On Camping script:

"Many thanks for the script. Very funny! I drove Val [his wife] potty laughing aloud. That doesn't often happen when one reads! There are some wonderful moments. So clean too."

526

Carry On Cruising was the first Carry On in colour, which meant the budget was £145,400, £30,000 more than the previous black and white Carry On, Carry On Regardless.

527

Alexandra Dane appears in five Carry On films: Carry On Doctor Carry On Up the Khyber, Carry On Again Doctor), Carry On Loving and Carry On Behind.

528

Renee Houston, who appears as Vic Spanner's Mother in Carry On at your Convenience, was going to play Miss Dukes in Carry On Girls. Unfortunately she could not appear due to health reasons. The role was played by Joan Hickson.

529

Marianne Stone appears in nine Carry On films: Carry On Nurse; Carry On Constable; Carry On Jack; Carry On Screaming!; Carry On Don't Lose Your Head; Carry On Doctor; Carry On at Your Convenience; Carry On Girls; Carry On Dick; Carry On Behind.

530

In Carry On Girls, Fircombe Town Hall is Slough Town Hall.

531

For Carry On Again Doctor, Jim Dale performed all his own stunts.

532

Barbara Windsor said in an interview that she was to play Cleopatra in Carry On Cleo, but refused to wear a black wig for the role. Producer Peter Rogers denied this.

533

Kenneth Williams said Carry On Cowboy was his favorite Carry On film.

534

The hospital party in Carry On Again Doctor was filmed in the lunchroom of Pinewood Studios.

535

The mostly Spanish set Carry On Abroad was filmed in England.

536

The Whippit Inn in Carry On At Your Convenience is Heatherden Hall in Pinewood Studios.

537

In Carry On Up The Jungle, Jacki Piper has a scene where water is thrown into her face. On the first take her wig and false eye lashes fell off.

538

There is a story that Barbara Windsor left the set of Carry On Emmannuelle as she did not like the more adult tone of the film. But, the story is untrue.

539

Sid James had suffered a small heart attack before Carry On Follow That Camel was filmed. His role was taken by Phil

Silvers.

540

Some alternative titles for Carry On Up The Jungle are:

"Carry On Tarzan" (Denmark), "Adventures in Africa" (Sweden), "Watch Out for the Jungle" (South America), "Queen of the Amazons" (Germany), "Full Speed Ahead Safari" (Poland) and "Carry On Through the Jungle" (Hungary).

541

In Carry On Loving, Richard O'Callaghan (Bertrum Muffet) was not on set during the filming of the food fight at the end of the film. His close up scenes were filmed separately and edited in.

542

Joan Sims called her role as Belle Armitage her favorite Carry on part.

543

In 1999, Carry On Up The Khyber was 99th on the British Film Institute's list of greatest British films ever made.

544

Carry On Cabby is the only Carry On film film that has both the Rank logo and the Anglo Amalgamated logo in the pre-credits.

545

Sid James was a fan of westerns and the Wild West as a child in South Africa; so he was pleased when he appeared in Carry On Cowboy.

546

Another comedy series similar to the Carry Ons in the Doctor series. The films were based on Richard Gordon's popular books about a group of young doctors. Seven films were made between 1954 and 1970. They were produced By Carry On Peter Rogers's wide Betty E. Box, and Carry On director Gerald Thomas's brother Peter Rogers. Seven television series based on the books were made.

547

In Carry On Henry, Barbara Windsor first appears after 54 minutes.

548

The Army HQ in Carry On England is Heatherden Hall in Pinewood Studios.

549

Charles Hawtrey's last Carry on film was Carry On Abroad. He was dropped from the series because he pulled out of the 1972 Christmas special, and his problems with alcohol.

550

In Carry On Henry, someone suggests that Henry have a cup

of tea. But tea was introduced to England more than 100 years after King Henry VIII's time.

551

Terry Scott had his scenes cut from the final version of Carry On At Your Convenience. Director Gerald Thomas wrote a letter to Terry:

"...this is in no way any reflection on you or your performance but the film finished fifty minutes over length and we felt rather than cut your sequence down so that you were only on the screen for a flash it would be kinder to remove the entire scene as really it had no effect one way or the other on the story, such as it is".

552

The Carry On Up the Khyber dinner scene was filmed in one take, which caused problems as no one could laugh at the other performers and ruin the take. Peter Butterworth made people laugh during the scene, and Angela Douglas had trouble containing her laughter, so there were no close ups of her during the scene.

553

Charles Hawtrey is one of the top billed names for Carry On Screaming! but only has about 5 minutes on screen.

554

In Carry On Matron Jane Darling's house is the White House in Denham Village, Buckinghamshire.

555

Carry On Cowboy has a cameo by Eric Rogers, the composer of the film's soundtrack. He appears as a band leader in the saloon bar.

556

Bernard Bresslaw was 6 ft 7 in (2.01 m). Barbara Windsor was 4 ft 10 in (1.47 m).

557

Carry On Again Doctor sees Kenneth Williams and Kenneth Connor appear in a Carry On together for the first time since Carry On Cleo which was made seven years earlier.

558

During the filming of Carry On Follow That Camel at Sahara Desert substitute Camber Sands in East Sussex, it started to snow. Director Gerald Thomas suggested putting a yellow filter on the camera to make the snow look like a sandstorm.

559

Charles Hawtrey appears 67 minutes into Carry On Up The Jungle.

560

Carry On At Your Convenience was known as Carry On Round The Bend outside Britain.

561

Carry On Cruising, the sixth film in the series, was the first to be filmed in colour.

562

Before become a director, Carry On director Gerald Thomas worked as a film editor.

563

Renee Houston had a temporary face lift during Carry On At Your Convenience: she got Jacki Piper to tape the back of her ears!

564

Carry On Cowboy is the first Carry On to have a person singing the theme song in the credits.

565

Sergeant Bung's car in Carry On Screaming is a 1904 Brushmobile, registration number HS 25. The company was based in Loughborough in Leicestershire, England. Only six of these cars were made.

566

In Carry On Follow That Camel, Bernard Bresslaw plays Abdul Abulbal. The name is based on Percy French's song Abdul Abulbul Amir.

567

John Antrobus and Brock Williams added material to the original script of Carry On Constable; but, their work did not make the final script.

568

Carry On Don't Lose Your Head and Carry On Follow That Camel were released with out the Carry On prefix after Rank took over distribution. The following film Carry On Doctor was going to have another non Carry On title - Nurse Carries On Again.

569

In the dinner scene at the end of Carry On Up the Khyber the diners are eating ham and boiled potatoes. Sid James did not eat ham as he was Jewish, so he is eating potatoes and gravy.

570

The road to the Elsbels Hotel in Carry On Abroad is located in Bagshot, Surrey.

571

In Carry On Camping, Sandra Caron, Anna Karen and Barbara Windsor play schoolgirls. All three actresses were over 30 years old.

572

The Helping Hands Agency in Carry On Regardless is located on Park Street in Windsor.

573

Carry On Up The Khyber is often called the Carry On by film critics and academics. For example, Colin MaCabe or the University of Exeter said in 1999 that Carry On Cleo and Carry On Up The Khyber "are two of the best films ever".

574

For Carry On Girls, Barbara Windsor had motorcycle lessons to film her scenes riding the motorbike on the pier.

575

In 2003, De Agostini released The Classic Carry On Film Collection series. Each magazine had a Carry On DVD or VHS tape. The magazines featured articles on the film associated with the specific magazine. Also a suitcase holder was provided to store the collection.

Thirty four magazine made up the series. Four episodes were devoted to the Carry On Laughing television series; Carry On Columbus was absent from the collection.

576

Talbot Rothwell signed a three film contract to write Carry On films, starting with Carry On Dick. Unfortunately he suffered from mental fatigue and eyestrain while writing the script. It was suggested he had overworked and needed a long rest. As a result he retired from scriptwriting.

577

Some alternate titles for Carry On Dick are:

"Go on Dick" (Hungary), "Carry on Robber" (Germany), "The Totally Crazy Mugger" (West Germany), "Do it again, Dick" (Eastern Germany [former GDR]) and "Way to Go...of Gurnard Unleashed" (Portugal).

578

Carry On Behind ran over the filming schedule and went over budget because of the awful weather during the shoot.

579

The Scottish actor Chic Murray was considered for the role of Sgt. Wilkins in Carry On Constable; the role went to Sid James.

581

The Chateau Neuf in Carry On Don't Lose Your Head is Waddesdon Manor, Near Aylesbury, Buckinghamshire.

582

Jack Douglas appears in eight Carry On films: Carry On Matron, Carry On Abroad, Carry On Girls, Carry On Dick, Carry On Behind, Carry On England (1976), Carry On Emmannuelle (1978) and Carry On Columbus (1992.

583

Kenneth Connor has the top billing in the cast list for Carry On Nurse and Carry On England.

584

When Talbot Rothwell told Sid James he was writing a

western Carry On, James asked to play the villain.

585

Carol Hawkins appears in Carry On Abroad and Carry On Behind as a glamorous young woman. She turned down Carry On England as her role featured nudity. The part went to Tricia Newby.

586

Carry On Abroad's opening credits feature Sun Tan Lo Tion as Technical Director.

587

In 1998 a Carry On documentary was made to celebrate the 40th Anniversary of the series. It is called What's a Carry On? The documentary featured interviews with surviving cast members, out takes and archive footage.

588

French actress Dany Robin, who appears in Carry On Don't Lose Your Head, owned five crocodiles and other animals at her farmhouse near Paris in France. She was also married to Sid James's agent.

589

Judy Geeson played Sergeant Tilly Willing in Carry On England. Her sister, Sally, appears in Carry On Girls, Carry On Abroad and Carry On Regardless.

590

Talbot Rothwell was paid £3000 for each script.

591

Carry On Camping receive an R rating in the US; this meant under 16's had to be accompanied by an adult.

592

Carry On Emmanuelle was Jack Douglas's first Carry appearance where did not wear his comedy glasses or do his twitching routine.

593

The map in Charlie's taxi office in Carry On Cabby is of Reading in Berkshire.

594

Special jewellery was bought from London for Fenella Fielding to wear in Carry On Screaming!. It matched her red dress. But, Fielding chose to wear a £9 ring of her own.

595

In Carry On Behind, Joe and Norma's house is on the Pinewood Green Estate.

596

Howard Nelson plays Harry Hernia in Carry On Emmannuelle. His voice was dubbed by Kenneth Connor.

597

Kenneth Williams, Eric Barker and Kenneth Connor are the only three actors who appear in the first Carry On, Carry On Sergeant in 1958, and Carry On Emmannuelle in 1978.

598

The room at Pinewood Studios used for the matchmaking agency in Carry On Loving was the same room used for the Helping Hands employment agency in Carry On Regardless (1961).

599

During the filming of Carry On Camping, Betty Marsden (who played Harriet Potter) was scared of riding the tandem bicycle.

600

The humour in the Carry Ons is similar to the humour of the British seaside postcard. These postcards were popular from the 1930s, and depict a cartoon with a risque joke, often based upon a double ententre or innuendo.

601

Carry On producer Peter Roger's favourite Carry on was Carry On Up The Khyber.

602

There were plans to film Carry On Cruising in Southampton and on a cruise in Gibraltar. But it was decided to film on a purpose built cruise ship set at Pinewood Studios.

603

In Carry On Camping, Amelia Bayntun plays Joan Sims's mother. Bayntun was only 11 years older.

604

These are the dates that the Carry On films were first shown in the cinema in Britain:

Carry On Sergeant 31st August 1958

Carry On Nurse 5th March 1959

Carry On Teacher 3rd September 1959

Carry On Constable 25 February 1960

Carry On Regardless 7 April 1961

Carry On Cruising 13 April 1962

Carry On Cabby 7 November 1963

Carry On Jack 23 February 1964

Carry On Spying 29 July 1964

Carry On Cleo December 10, 1964

Carry On Cowboy 26 November 1965

Carry On Screaming 2 March 1967

Don't Lose Your Head 16 August 1966

Follow That Camel 14 December 1967

Carry On Doctor March 1968

Carry On Up the Khyber November 28, 1968

Carry On Camping 29 May 1969

Carry On Again Doctor 2 December 1969

Carry On Loving September 1970

Carry On Henry February 1971

Carry On At Your Convenience 10 December 1971

Carry On Matron 19 May 1972

Carry On Abroad 15 December 1972

Carry On Girls 9 November 1973

Carry On Dick 12 July 1974

Carry On Behind 19 December 1975

Carry On England 31 October 1976

That's Carry On November 1977

Carry On Emmannuelle 24 November 1978

Carry On Columbus October 1992

605

In Carry On Girls, the town Fircombe is pronounced Firk-em. Mrs Prodworthy says Fircoom. A deleted scene saw Mrs Prodworthy explain that her innuendo free pronunciation is the correct one.

606

In Carry On Regardless, Joan Sims actually drinks real gin in the wine tasting scene. Director Gerald Thomas put the gin in place of the non-alcoholic drink to get a good reaction shot from Sims!

607

The location filming for Carry On Follow That Camel at Camber Sands in East Sussex took three weeks. This was the longest location filming in the series.

608

In the scene in Carry On Henry where Henry (Sid James) is chases out of a barn by a girl's father it is a double who is running off and not Sid James.

609

The bronze statues of a woman holding a clock on W.C. Boggs's fireplace in Carry On At Your Convenience came from The Private Life of Sherlock Holmes.

610

One of the ideas for the title of Carry On Follow That Camel was Carry On Bo.

611

When Carry On Behind was being filmed at Pinewood, Bernard and Joan Sims also filmed another film at Pinewood at the same time. The film was One of Our Dinosaurs is Missing.

612

The British censor had a problem with Bungdit Din's line "Fakir, off" in Carry On Up The Khyber. The censor said there had to be a noticeable pause between fakir and off.

613

It took three takes to film the famous scene in Carry On Camping where Barbara Windsor's bra flies off during the exercise scene. The first two takes saw Barbara fall in the mud and the second saw her "right boob" revealed. In the end, the censor passed the "right boob" take. He said: 'Well, I don't think Miss Windsor's right boob is going to corrupt the nation, I'll pass it.'

614

Gerald Thomas's older brother Ralph Thomas co-directed Carry On Regardless, but was uncredited.

615

A frame of the end shot of Carry On Cowboy is used in series two of BBC television sitcom The Young Ones.

616

The filming dates for the Carry Ons were:

Carry On Sergeant 24 March – 2 May 1958

Carry On Nurse 3 November – 12 December 1958

Carry On Teacher March – 45 April 1959

Carry On Constable 9 November - 18 December 1959

Carry On Regardless 28 November 1960 – 17 January 1961

Carry On Cruising 28 November 1960 – 17 January 1961

Carry On Cabby 25 March – 7 May 1963

Carry On Jack 2 September – 26 October 1963

Carry On Spying 8 February –13 March 1964

Carry On Cleo 13 July – 28 August 1964

Carry On Cowboy 12 July – 3 September 1965

Carry On Screaming 10 January – 25 February 1966

Don't Lose Your Head 12 September - 28 October 1966

Follow That Camel 1 May- 23 June 1967

Carry On Doctor 11 September - 20 October 1967

Carry On Up the Khyber 8 April - 31 May 1968

Carry On Camping 7 October – 22 November 1968

Carry On Again Doctor 17 March - 2 May 1969

Carry On Up the Jungle 13 October - 21 November 1969

Carry On Loving 6 April - 15 May 1970

Carry On Henry 12 October -27 November 1970

Carry On At Your Convenience 22 March - 7 May 1971

Carry On Matron 11 October - 26 November 1971

Carry On Abroad 17 April - 26 May 1972

Carry On Girls 16 April - 25 May 1973

Carry On Dick 4 March - 11 April 1974

Carry On Behind 10 March – 18 April 1975

Carry On England 3 May - 4 June 1976

Carry On Emmannuelle 10 April - 15 May 1978

Carry On Columbus 21 April – 27 May 1992

617

The coach trip to Brighton in Carry On At Your Convenience was filmed near the end of the shoot, from Monday the 3rd May to Wednesday the 6th May.

618

During the bombardment scene in Carry On Up the Khyber where the British Consulate is attacked, a broken window and blind behind the piano magically become repaired

619

Carry On Up The Jungle is missing a number of Carry On stars. These include Kenneth Williams Hattie Jacques, Peter Butterworth and Barbara Windsor.

620

Carry On At Your Convenience is rare in that it contains a dramatic emotional scene. Sid Plummer and Chloe Moore (Sid James and Joan Sims) discuss whether they could have an affair outside their houses.

621

Some other titles for Carry On Screaming! are:

"Frankenstein Junior" (Greece), "With Pointed Teeth" (South America), "Alarm in a Creepy Castle" (Germany) and "Between the Crazy Monsters" (Turkey).

622

In 1962, Norman Hudis wrote a Carry On script about Royal Air Force recruits. It was called Carry On Flying, and was based on Hudis's experiences in the RAF during World War 2. Producer Peter Rogers did not go ahead with the film as he thought there was the possibility of an air disaster occurring during the release of the film.

623

In Carry On at Your Convenience, an extra plays both a man in the cinema and a factory worker.

624

Kenneth Williams was looking forward to filming Carry On Cruising as he thought the film would be shot in the Mediterranean. But, of course, it was all filmed at Pinewood Studios.

625

Carry On Camping was released in 1969. But, scriptwriter Talbot Rothwell first wrote the script in 1962. It was decided to make Carry On Cruising instead, and Carry On Camping was eventually made later on.

626

In Carry On Up The Jungle, it was planned to have Professor Tinkle's lecture to be longer and for him to introduce the other characters.

627

The last line in Carry On Cabby, spoken by Charlie (Sid James) is "Call me a cab". Call Me a Cab was going to be the title of the film.

628

During the filming of Carry On At Your Convenience, Bill Maynard (Fred Moore) was appearing on stage in Wolverhampton in the play The Ghost Train.

629

The Grubb family house in Carry On Loving is on Queens Road in Windsor.

630

The writers of BBC radio comedy, The Navy Lark, were asked to write a navy set Carry On by Peter Rogers in the 1970s. Laurie Wyman and George Evans wrote a script called Carry On Sailor, but it was not used.

631

In Carry On At Your Convenience, Terry Scott played Mr Allcock, the trade union leader. Unfortunately his scenes were deleted.

632

Carry On Spying was the first in the series to star Barbara Windsor.

633

Some other titles for Carry On Cleo were:

"Ok, Cleo" (Belgium), "So, So Cleopatra" (Denmark), "Stop Your Chariot Cleo" (France), "Way to Go Cleopatra"

(Portugal), and "Heroic Suckers in the Country of the Pharaoh" (Greece).

634

Norman Hudis was going to write the script for Carry On Matron (1972). But, he was working in the US and a member of the Writers' Guild of America. This made it difficult for him to work on a script for a British film. Talbot Rothwell wrote the script.

635

Ted Ray starred as the headmaster in Carry On Teacher. Ray was a very popular radio personality and a success in his Carry On role. It was planned that he would feature in more Carry Ons. But, he was under contract to a rival film company ABC. ABC threatened the Carry On production team with legal action and as a result Ray only made one Carry On film.

636

In Carry On Cruising, chef Wilfred Haines comically puts lots of eggs in a metal pot, drops the pot to break the eggs, then drains the eggs to remove the shell. This technique for breaking eggs is actually used.

637

Carry On Up the Khyber is set in 1895. In the film, Sir Sidney Ruff-Diamond dictates a letter to Queen Victoria and says "PS, Love to Albert". Prince Albert died in 1861.

638

The castle's gardens in Carry On Henry are in Pinewood Studios.

639

In Carry On Up The Jungle Joan Sims plays Lady Evelyn, the father of Cecil The Jungle Boy, played by Terry Scott. Sims was three years older than Terry Scott.

640

It was planned for Barbara Windsor to appear in Carry On Emmannuelle playing four different characters in fantasy dream sequences. But, she was appearing in a play and unavailable for the film.

641

Frankie Howerd was asked to play Dr Watt in Carry On Screaming!. But, Howerd was not available for filming.

642

Charles Hawtrey was going to be called James Bind in Carry On Spying. But the producer of the James Bond films thought this name was too close to James Bond and threatened legal action. In the end, Hawtrey's character was called Charlie Bind.

643

Jack Douglas did not receive a fee for Carry On Columbus.

644

Peter Rogers wanted George Cole (best known for his role as Arthur Daley in television series Minder) for the role of Charlie in Carry On Sergeant. Bob Monkhouse played the role.

645

Here is a list of Carry On films by year:

1958

Carry On Sergeant

1959

Carry On Nurse
Carry On Teacher

1960

Carry On Constable

1961

Carry On Regardless
1962

Carry On Cruising

1963

Carry On Cabby
Carry On Jack

1964

Carry On Spying
Carry On Cleo

1965

Carry On Cowboy
Carry On Screaming!

1966

Carry On Don't Lose Your Head

1967

Carry On Follow That Camel
Carry On Doctor

1968

Carry On Up The Khyber (1968)

1969

Carry On Camping (1969)
Carry On Again Doctor (1969)

1970

Carry On Up The Jungle (1970)
Carry On Loving (1970)

1971

Carry On Henry (1971)
Carry On At Your Convenience (1971)

1972

Carry On Matron (1972)
Carry On Abroad (1972)

1973

Carry On Girls (1973)

1974

Carry On Dick (1974)

1975

Carry On Behind (1975)

1976

Carry On England (1976)

1978

That's Carry On (1978)
Carry On Emmannuelle (1978)

1992

Carry On Columbus (1992)

646

When Charles Hawtrey sleeps in the tent with Terry Scott and Betty Marsden in Carry On Camping, he is in a blue sleeping bag. In the morning it has turned into one with a flower pattern.

647

Long Hampton Hospital in Carry On Again Doctor is Maidenhead Town Hall.

648

Billy Cornelius said that Charles Hawtrey would bring a big bag of "goodies" on set and carry it around with him.

649

Actor Patrick Newell - who played Mother in the Avengers television series - originally cast for Carry On Sergeant. He had done National Service with Michael Caine. When he arrived for filming he left the film because the army sergeant provided for the film was the one who had drilled him and been horrible to him in National Service!

650

The final image at the end of Carry On Up the Khyber is a shot of the British Union Flag with the phrase "I'm backing Britain". "I'm backing Britain" was a government campaign to get people to buy British goods.

651

In 2007, Sky Movies conducted a poll of the funniest one line joke in film history. Julius's Caesar's (Kenneth Williams) line "Infamy, infamy, they've all got it in for me" was voted number 1.

The Life of Brian quote "He's not the Messiah, he's a very naughty boy" was second.

Leslie Nielsen's line from Airplane! "don't call me Shirley" came third.

652

Carry On Emmannuelle was the first Carry On in which the cast were credited at the end of the film.

653

At the start of Carry On Cruising, the shadow of the boom microphone can be seen on the chef's hat.

654

Bill Maynard sadly had his role in Carry On Abroad as Wundertours owner Mr Fiddler cut.

655

In Carry On Cowboy, Sheriff Earp's (Jon Pertwee) glasses have a hole in the middle, so Pertwee could see through the thick glass.

656

In Carry On Camping, Miss Haggard (Hattie Jacques) refers to her previous job in a hospital, which may refer to Carry On doctor.

657

In Carry On Cruising, stock footage of the P&O cruise ship S.S. Oronsay is used for some exteriors and long shots at sea.

658

Kenneth Williams did not appear in the Carry On Christmas television specials or the Carry On Laughing television series.

659

Peter Gilmore appears in eleven Carry On films:

Carry On Cabby, Carry On Jack, Carry On Cleo), Carry On Cowboy, Carry On Don't Lose Your Head, Carry On Follow That Camel, Carry On Doctor, Carry On Up The Khyber, Carry On Again Doctor, Carry On Henry and Carry On Columbus

660

William Hartnell appears in one Carry On film: Carry On Sergeant.

661

Some of Dr Crow's female staff have hairstyles similar to those of the London Evening Standard cartoon character Modesty Blaise.

662

Charles Hawtrey appears in twenty-three Carry On films:

Carry On Sergeant, Carry On Nurse, Carry On Teacher, Carry On Constable, Carry On Regardless, Carry On Cabby Carry On Jack, Carry On Spying, Carry On Cleo, Carry On Cowboy, Carry On Screaming, Carry On Don't Lose Your Head, Carry On Follow That Camel, Carry On Doctor, Carry On Up the Khyber, Carry On Camping, Carry On Again Doctor, Carry On Loving , Carry On Henry, Carry On Up the Jungle, Carry On at Your Convenience, Carry On Matron and Carry On Abroad.

Also appeared in the 1969 and 1970 television Carry On Christmas specials.

663

Windsor Davies plays a Sergeant Major in Carry On England who is very similar to the popular Sergeant Major character he plays in BBC sitcom It Ain't Half Hot Mum. It Ain't Half Hot Mum ran from 1974-1981.

664

The entrance to the campsite in Carry On Camping is the entrance to Dromenagh Farm, Sevenhills Road, Iver Heath, Buckingham; the farm is very near to Pinewood Studios

665

Jill Ireland appears in one Carry On film: Carry On Nurse.

666

The helter skelter and ghost train in Carry On At Your Convenience were located on the Palace Pier in Brighton. The Palace Pier is now the Brighton Pier. The original Ghost Train was destroyed in a fire, but a ghost train is operating on the Pier today.

667

The Citizen's Advice Bureau in Carry On Loving is on Frances Road in Windsor, Berkshire.

668

Sid James appears in nineteen of the Carry On films:

Carry On Constable, Carry On Regardless, Carry On Cruising, Carry On Cabby, Carry On Cleo, Carry On Cowboy, Carry On Don't Lose Your Head, Carry On Doctor, Carry On Up the Khyber, Carry On Camping, Carry On Again Doctor, Carry On Up the Jungle, Carry On Loving, Carry On Henry, Carry On at Your Convenience, Carry On Matron, Carry On Abroad, Carry On Girls and Carry On Dick.

He appeared in the Carry On London stage show in 1973, the 1969, 1970 and 1973 Carry On Christmas specials, and the Carry On Laughing television series.

669

The Citizen's Advice Bureau in Carry On Loving is on Frances Road in Windsor.

670

Dilys Laye appears in four Carry On films:

Carry On Cruising, Carry On Spying, Carry On Doctor and Carry On Camping.

671

In Carry On Girls Mildred Bumble is always smoking; but the actress who play Mildred, Patsy Rowlands, did not smoke.

672

The Army Camp in Carry On England is in Pinewood Studios orchard.

673

Terence Longdon appears in four Carry On films: Carry On Sergeant, Carry On Nurse, Carry On Constable and Carry On Regardless.

674

The role of Brigadier in Carry On England is played by Peter Jones. The role was written for Kenneth Williams, but he was appearing in the stage play Signed and Sealed and was not available.

675

In Carry On Teacher, real itching powder was used in the itching powder attack on the staffroom.

676

The police station in Carry On Screaming is on St. Leonard's Road in Windsor. At the time of filming the building was Windsor's fire station; now the building is an arts centre.

677

Richard O'Callaghan appears in two Carry On films Carry On Loving and Carry On at Your Convenience.

678

It was decided to drop Charles Hawtrey from the series after Carry On Cowboy because his alcoholism was causing problems on set. But, as he was popular with audiences he was brought back for Carry On Screaming!

679

Terry Scott appears in seven Carry On films: Carry On Sergeant, Carry On Up The Khyber, Carry On Camping, Carry On Loving, Carry On Up The Jungle, Carry On Henry and Carry On Matron.

Also appears in the Carry on Christmas specials in 1969 and 1970.

680

Jacki Piper left the Carry series after 1972's Carry On Matron as she was pregnant with her first son, Tim.

681

In Carry On Camping, a scene in the script had Kenneth Williams have an altercation with a roadside cafe owner on the way to the campsite, but the scene was cut.

682

Ted Ray appears in one Carry On film: Carry on Teacher.

683

Jack Douglas says he was able to do what he wanted with his twitching character William in Carry On Girls.

684

There is a story that Sid James filmed a cameo for Carry On Behind, but no such scene exists.

685

Julian Holloway called Carry On Camping a "miserable shoot".

686

For Margaret Nolan's nude scene with Robin Askwith on Brighton beach in Carry On Girls, four policemen acted as bodyguards.

687

Joan Sims appears in 24 Carry On films:

Carry On Nurse, Carry On Teacher, Carry On Constable, Carry On Regardless, Carry On Cleo, Carry On Cowboy, Carry On Screaming, Carry On Don't Lose Your Head, Carry On Follow That Camel, Carry On Doctor, Carry On Up the Khyber, Carry On Camping, Carry On Again Doctor, Carry On Up the Jungle,

Carry On Loving, Carry On Henry, Carry On at Your Convenience, Carry On Matron, Carry On Abroad, Carry On Girls, Carry On Dick, Carry On Behind, Carry On England and Carry On Emmannuelle.

She appears in the 1972 and 1973 Carry On Christmas television specials, and the Carry On Laughing television series.

688

Leslie Phillips appears in four Carry On films: Carry On Nurse, Carry On Teacher, Carry On Constable and the last Carry On, Carry On Columbus.

689

The marriage in Carry On Don't Lose Your Head takes place at Denham Church near Iver Heath, Buckinghamshire.

690

During the filming of Carry On Loving, Jacki Piper and Richard O'Callaghan were appearing in separate theatre shows in London's West End in the evenings.

691

The Balsworth Youth Hostel in Carry On Camping is in Pinewood Studios.

692

Fenella Fielding was offered a role in Carry On Camping, but did not like the look of the script.

693

The Clarges Hotel in Brighton was used for the exterior scenes in Carry On Girls. The hotel was owned by Dora Bryan who appears in the first Carry On, Carry On Sergeant.

694

Julian Holloway said he was offered a role in Carry On Abroad, but turned it down. The casting director said he would never work with producer Peter Rogers again. But, Holloway did subsequently appear in the Carry On television series and Carry On England.

695

Carry On Spying had a budget £148,000. The first James Bond film Dr No had a budget of budget was £392,022.

696

One proposed title for Carry On England was Carry On Banging. Poster art with the Carry On Banging title were produced.

697

Julian Holloway said this about the Carry Ons in an interview: "I am not remotely proud of my involvement in the films.".

698

Sid drops Joan off in Carry On At Your Convenience at their houses in Pinewood Green Housing Estate.

699

In Carry On Girls, fairy liquid (dish soap) was put on the ramp at the beauty contest at the end of the film, so the models were falling over for real.

700

There is a rumour that Kenneth Cope appears in Carry On Jack as a sailor; but he denied this in an interview.

701

Melvyn Hayes accepted a part in Carry On England as he wanted to say he had been in a Carry On film.

702

Peter Rogers and Gerald Thomas said about the casting for Carry On Columbus that their first choice would be the original cast members, the second choice would be known actors, the third choice - anyone who would do it!

703

Anita Harris appears in two Carry On films: Follow That Camel and Carry On Doctor.

704

Producer Peter Rogers had this to say about shooting a Carry On film:

"We liked to keep our friends together. We almost had a repertory you see. And the same applied to the crew. We had almost the same electricians and people on each picture. In make up and hairdressing, when a couple of them retired and when we were making another Carry On, they asked if they could come back and do it. So we had the same people with us all the time".

705

In Carry On Regardless, Yoki the Chimp started smashing the ornaments in house during filming. Yoki's owners had to spend two hours calming him down.

706

The Carry On films did not get good review from film critics; but they were popular with audiences.

707

A film was made in 1957 called Carry On Admiral. It was a comedy and had Joan Sims in it, but the film has no connection the Carry On series or producers.

708

When Sergeant Bung drives his car in Carry On Screaming!, the theme from police television drama Z Cars is played.

709

Boxer Lefty Vincent in Carry On Regardless was played by real life boxer Freddie Mills, who was the World Light Heavyweight champion.

710

Carry On Laughing's Christmas Classics was shown on television at Christmas 1983. It was made by Thames TV (ITV). This was a Christmas special of the Carry On Laughing television series and was a compilation of classic clips from the films, with some new linking material with Kenneth Williams and Barbara Windsor.

711

Producer Peter Rogers said that author Nina Hibbin was "rude" about Carry On At Your Convenience as she was a Communist and did not like the attack on the Trade Unions in the film. "She subscribed to the Communist Party and she hated the idea and that was personal and she should never have put it in the book.", Rogers stated.

712

Khyber in Carry On Up The Khyber is short for Khyber Pass. Khyber Pass is cockney rhyming slang for arse/ass.

713

Simon Callow had his role deleted from the Orgy and Bess episode of the Carry On Laughing television series.

714

Derek Francis appears in six Carry On films: Carry On Camping, Carry On Henry, Carry On Doctor, Carry On Matron, Carry On Loving and Carry On Abroad.

715

The Republic of Ireland banned the scene where Barbara Windsor's bra flew off in Carry On Camping.

716

Patsy Rowlands said that the shoes she wore in the hospital scenes In Carry On Girls hurt her feet really badly.

717

Joan Hickson appears in five Carry On films: Carry On Nurse, Carry On Constable, Carry On Regardless, Carry On Loving and Carry On Girls.

718

The Caffin Ward Carry On Doctor was named after costume designer Yvonne Caffin.

719

Charles Hawtrey was cast as the music master in Carry On Teacher. Hawtrey was a boy soprano and classically trained pianist.

720

Brian Osborne appears in six Carry Ons: Carry On Matron, Carry On Abroad, Carry On Girls, Carry On Dick, Carry On Behind, and Carry On England.

721

Charles Hawtrey was 43 when he appeared in Carry On Sergeant, his first Carry On, and 57 when he appeared in his last - Carry On Abroad.

722

Julian Holloway says he appeared in Carry On England as he "needed the money".

723

Eric Barker appears in four Carry On film: Carry On Sergeant, Carry On Constable, Carry On Spying and Carry On Emmannuelle.

724

Joan Sim's favourite dish for lunch when filming a Carry On was shepherd's pie.

725

Juliet Mills said she receive better acting opportunities after appearing in Carry On Jack.

726

Joan Sims refused to attend the end of shoot party for Carry On Behind and went home as she was annoyed at the weather and delays in the schedule. Kenneth Connor had to fetch her and bring her back for the party,

727

Penelope Keith had her role as a nurse in Carry On Doctor cut.

728

Michael Ward appears in five Carry On films: Carry On Regardless, Carry On Cabby, Carry On Cleo, Carry On Screaming, and Carry On Don't Lose Your Head.

729

The toilet factory workers on the outing to Brighton enjoy the amusements on the Palace Pier in Brighton. This is now called the Brighton Pier.

730

Percy Herbert appears in two Carry On films: Carry On Jack and Carry On Cowboy.

731

Talbot Rothwell became ill writing the 1972 Carry On Christmas television special, Carry On Stuffing. Dave Freeman completed the script.

732

Barbara Windsor missed Carry On At Your Convenience. She was especially wanted for a leading role Carry On Matron to win back cinemagoers who had not watched Carry On At Your Convenience, which was a flop.

733

The 1972 Carry On Christmas television special, Carry On Stuffing, featured two madrigals (a type of vocal music) written for Carry On Henry. The madrigals also appeared in the Carry On London stage show.

734

Betty Marsden appears in two Carry On films: Carry On Regardless and Carry On Camping.

735

Joan Sims and Kenneth Williams had a shouting match during Carry On Again Doctor. Hattie Jacques stopped it by telling Williams off.

736

June Jago appears in two Carry On films: Carry On Regardless and Carry On Doctor.

737

Diane Langton appears in two Carry On films: Carry On Teacher and Carry On England.

She also appears in three episodes of the Carry On Laughing television series.

738

The Carry On Laughing television series episode Orgy and Bess saw the last ever Carry On performances of Sid James and

Hattie Jacques.

739

Carry On scriptwriter Talbot Rothwell used some jokes and comic dialogues from the BBC radio series Take It from here when he ran out of time when writing the scripts. Take It from here writers Frank Muir and Denis Norden gave Rothwell some old scripts to use.

740

In 1983 a Carry On television clip show was made called Carry On Laughing's Christmas Classics. Kenneth Williams and Barbara Windsor filmed new material introducing the clips.

741

Marian Collins appears in four Carry On films, all in uncredited roles: Carry On Cruising, Carry On Cabby, Carry On Jack and Carry On Spying.

742

The Drayton Court Hotel in Eailing, London, can be seen in many scenes in Carry On Constable.

743

Hattie Jacques received a fee of £100 for her small role in Carry On Regardless.

744

Carry On Cabby was based on a stage play called Call Me a Cab. This was going to be the title of the film, but it was decided to make it a Carry On film.

745

When Carry On Abroad is shown on British television, the scenes where the chief of police sticks two finger up at Stuart Farqhuar, a shot of Sadie's bum in the shower and Vic pulling Sadie's top off are cut out.

746

The department store in Carry On Constable was the F.H. Rowse department store. The building was demolished in the early 1980s. It was located on the junction of Green Man Lane and Uxbridge Road in Ealing, London.

747

Lance Percival makes his only appearance in the series in Carry On Cruising

748

Sid James could not appear in Carry On Follow That Camel as he was working on his ITV television sitcom George and the Dragon. At the time Carry On Follow that Camel was being filmed, James suffered his first heart attack.

749

Carry On Nurse made over £2 million in the cinema in the US.

750

Scenes for Carry On Constable were filmed near the Royal Mail Sorting Office and the railway footbridge in Ealing, London.

751

Popular American actor Phil Silvers was cast in Carry On Follow That Camel on try to increase the popularity of the Carry Ons in the US.

752

Carry On spying spoofs spy films such as The Third Man and the James Bond films. Eric Pohlman plays the Fat Man in Carry On spying; he also has a part in The Third Man and was the voice of SPECTRE No 1 in From Russia With Love.

753

Imogen Hassell appeared in one Carry On film: Carry On Loving (1970).

754

Talbot Rothwell did not come up with the line from Carry On Cleo "Infamy, infamy, they've all got it in for me", spoken by Kenneth Williams.

He got permission to use it from Frank Muir and Denis Norden, who wrote it for an episode of the BBC radio comedy Take It from here.

755

Angela Douglas sings This is the Night for Love in the saloon bar in Carry On Cowboy.

756

Carry On constable filmed scenes at the parade of shops on The Avenue, West Ealing, London.

757

Academic Colin MaCabe had this to say about the Carry On series:

"In many ways the Carry Ons are like the Wodehouse novels: they produce an imaginary and coherent vision of an England that never existed but in which we can all feel at home. It is perhaps no surprise that their great period coincided exactly with the Wilson government, another sustained exercise in wishful thinking. The advent of the Heath government signalled a terrible decline. The Carry Ons depended on censorship and repression and could not long survive the permissive society of the seventies. They limped through most of that decade before expiring with the dreadful Carry On Emmanuelle (1978). The attempt to revive them with Carry On Columbus (1992) only proved how dependent they were on their original stars and context."

758

When Carry On Screaming! Aired on British television over Easter in 2023, all of Dan Dann's scenes were cut out. So, Charles Hawtrey had fourth billing in the film, but did not appear on screen at all!

759

ITV made a television documentary on the Carry On films in 2015. Titles Carry On Forever, the three part retrospective was narrated by Martin Clunes. The documentary featured unseen footage and looked at the Carry On films in order. Surviving Carry On cast members share their memories of making the films.

760

Bertie Muffet looks into a window in Carry On Loving on the High Street in Windsor.

761

Jim Dale thought he had ruined his chances of working on a Carry On film when he appeared in the 1961 comedy Raising the Wind, which was made by the Carry On team and featured many Carry On stars.

Dale had one line in the film with Kenneth Williams, and delivered his line in Williams's voice. Kenneth was angry, and Dale thought he would not be wanted in a Carry On. But, he was asked to appear in Carry On Cabby in 1963. Williams had said to the casting director about the incident in Raising the Wind 'Use him [Dale], for god's sake. If he can take the mickey out of me and make me laugh, he's worth a bloody fortune for you."

762

Kenneth Williams did not like Charles Hawtrey because of Hawtrey's unreliability and alcoholism.

763

Jacki Piper had this to say about Hattie Jacques:

"She was like a walking cream cake...she was just lovely. She and I hated seeing ourselves on screen... so she and I used to rush off to the tea trolley and eat bacon sarnies instead of watching the rushes."

764

Jim Dale said he wished Hattie Jacques had more funny lines: "She was a very, very funny lady. I only wish they'd given her more joke lines. She used to just be the one who threw lines at Kenneth and he got the punchline.

765

Joan Sims had a body double for her shower scenes in Carry On Up The Jungle. Jacki Piper recalls Joan laughing at the stand in:

"She was supposed to be having a shower naked in the jungle, with little bits of her being seen. Of course, she wasn't. She had a body stand-in. She sat next to me saying, 'Ooooh haven't I got a lovely body... Nice bum.' She was making me scream with laughter."

766

Jim Dale said that there was no improvisation allowed on the Carry On set:

"Everyone had to be word perfect for that script. That script had been edited, edited, edited – and you were not allowed to improvise, as they often are today. It was very disciplined on that set. They were very reluctant to do more than one due to the cost of real film in those days."

767

Marytn Hesford wrote Fantabulosa, a television film about the life of Kenneth Williams. He had this to say about the Carry On films:

"There was a great snobbery about the Carry Ons at the time. It was only in the 1980s when they were rediscovered by BBC Two and Channel 4 and intellectualised to a certain degree. In the 1960s they were frowned upon: these were lewd, rude jokes."

768

Sid James said in an interview that he was always recognised around the world from his role in the Carry On films. In Bangkok he recalls: "We get to the passport bloke and he gets a funny look on his face and says, 'Carry On Camping.'"

769

In the scene in Carry On Abroad where Vic is having a coffee outside the hotel and Cora says "Don't bother to ask me if I'd like a chair", a microphone can be seen in the bottom left hand corner of the screen.

770

During the filming of Carry On At Your Convenience, Kenneth Williams was appearing in the evening in the West End of London in George Bernard Shaw's play Captain Brassbound's

Conversion with Ingrid Bergman. Kenneth had Sundays off from the Carry On film filming and the play. But, he did not have the Sunday off as he was compering the BBC television variety show Meanwhile on BBC2.

771

Jacki Piper asked Carry On producer Peter Rogers for a car to take her to set each morning. Rogers said:

"Well, Miss Piper. You can either have a car and no money, or money and no car."

772

Carry On producer Peter Rogers had this to say about the prospect of more Carry On films in 1997:

"...first of all so many of the cast are not here anymore, although one can start again with the Ian Lavenders, and Davenports and all those sorts of people that are on television. It's a question of cost today because the margin is so narrow now and films are so expensive to make. Columbus was a very expensive film. I would like to do Carry On specials for television, that's what I would really like to do. I can't see people queuing in the rain in Wigan to go and see a Carry On but I can see them enjoying them on television."

773

In Carry On Screaming, Sgt. Bung's house is located on Queens Road in Windsor.

774

In Carry On Teacher, Mr Bean conducts the orchestra and the school crest can be seen on the stage curtain. The crest has the phrase: "Continua O Domine", Latin for "Carry On, O Lord."

775

Charles Hawtrey turned down his part as Mr Bedsop in Carry Loving as he was not to have third billing as he had a small role; Hattie Jacques was to have had the third billing as she had a larger role.

But, in the end Peter Roger's gave Hawtrey third billing and he appeared in the film.

776

The Australian VHS release for Carry On Abroad says Elsbels is located in the Costa Plonka. Costa Plonka was not mentioned in Carry On Abroad, but was the setting for the 1977 Are You Being Served? film which was set in Spain.

777

Joan Sims was not a fan of her character's name in Carry On Again Doctor – Ellen Moore. It was plain compared to some other character names such as Dr Jimmy Nookey and Gladstone Screwer.

778

For three films, actors received a special billing in the credits: Ted Ray in Carry On Teacher, Bob Monkhouse in Carry On

Sergeant and Phil Silvers in Carry On Follow That Camel.

779

Carry Emmannuelle had a rating of AA in Britain, restricting the film to those aged 14 and over.

780

For Carry On Cabby there were promotional tie ins with the Ford Motor Company and Regent Petrol; both companies are featured in the film.

781

Charles Hawtrey and Kenneth Connor appear in the first scene ever filmed for a Carry On. The scene is a conversation in the mess in Carry On Sergeant.

782

Trisha Noble, who played Sally in Carry On Camping, caused problems on the set of Carry On Camping as she was always late.

783

Carry On Camping was the most popular film at the British box office in 1969.

784

After Carry On Regardless, producer Peter Rogers asked Talbot Rothwell to write a script. Rothwell wrote a script based around a campsite. Rogers decided to make Carry Cruising instead, and or course the camping themed film was eventually made as Carry On Camping.

785

In a 2007 poll asking which is the best Carry On film in British newspaper The Daily Mirror saw Carry On Camping voted the favourite.

786

Anglo-Amalgamated Production distributed first twelve Carry On films from 1958-66. The company stopped distributing the films as they wanted to distribute more serious films.

787

Bill Owen was paid £320 for 4 days work on Carry On Cabby.

788

Jacki Piper said that Carry On Up The Jungle was her favourite Carry On film.

789

Kenneth Williams was mostly critical of Sid James, but in his diary he praised James's performance in Carry On Cowboy

790

When Sid James was cast in Carry On Cowboy, he practiced a quick draw of a gun using a toy gun and holster.

791

Ernest Steward was the Director of Photography on ten Carry Ons, starting with Carry On Up the Khyber and ending with Carry On England.

792

The Charlton Heston film Khartoum (1966) is spoofed in Carry On Up the Khyber.

793

The highest grossing film at the British box office in 1969 was Carry On Camping.

794

Bernard Bresslaw told producer Peter Rogers that he could ride a motorcycle for scenes in Carry On At Your Convenience. But he could not.

795

Carry On Camping was refused a cinema certificate in the Republic of Ireland.

796

The original title for Carry On Girls was Carry On Beauty Queens.

797

The hippies who dance at the end of Carry On Camping were

extras from a local village to the set.

798

During the filming of a stunt in Carry On Again Doctor, Jim Dale's arm banged against a hospital trolley and he had to have an emergency operation. The next day he was back at work

799

In Britain, the posters for Carry On At Your Convenience reference the foreign title Carry On Round the Bend. The posters had the line: "The CARRY ON team carries on round the bend!".

800

Brian Wilde played a prison warder in Carry On Henry, but the scene was cut.

801

John Clive appeared as a dandy of the court in Carry On Henry, but the scene was cut.

802

During one of the takes of the famous Carry On Camping scene where the bra flies off, Barbara Windsor fell in the mud.

803

The coach scenes of the return from Brighton in Carry On At Your Convenience was filmed in Iver Heath and other local roads near Pinewood Studios.

804

Despite injuring himself in a stunt during the filming of Carry On Again Doctor, Jim Dale refused a stunt double for subsequent stunts.

805

Jim Dale appeared in Carry On Columbus as a favour to director Gerald Thomas.

806

Peter Butterworth sadly died two months after filming his scenes for Carry On Emmannuelle.

807

Kenneth Williams said this in his diaries about Carry On Emmannuelle:

"Gerald Thomas [director] gave me lunch. He talked to me about the Carry On Emmannuelle script; it sounds pretty dirty. 'We really miss old Sid James,' he said, 'he was cuddly & warm' (you could have fooled me) 'and there are so few like him.' Then he saw Jimmy Tarbuck at another table and said 'He'd got that quality!' & I said 'Yes! he is cuddly & warm & I think he's smashing...'"

808

Carry On England had a more adult certificate because of topless scenes and a joke about Fokker aircraft. But a cut version was re-released into cinemas.

809

In Carry On Behind Peter Butterworth plays a dishevelled campsite owner, which is the same character he plays in Carry On Camping.

810

Kenneth Williams said this in his diary about Carry On Dick: "I walked to Peter Eade [his agent] and read the script of Carry On Dick – said I'd do it if they cut the stocks scene (where I'm pelted with rubbish) and pay the salary after the tax period, ie April 6th. The script is utterly banal. It is incredible that human minds can put such muck on to paper." –

811

The Carry On Girls plot is based in the 1970 Miss World competition where feminist protesters threw flour bombs on the stage.

812

Barbara Windsor was surprised when she first heard she would be topless in the Carry On Camping bra exercise scene:

"I was so terrified. You weren't allowed to show your boobs.

813

Charles Hawtrey was cast in Carry On Christmas for 1972. But, he demanded top billing as Sid James was absent. The producers refused and Hawtrey pulled out at the last minute.

Hawtrey never worked in Carry On Again.

814

The all in trip to the Spanish resort of Els Bels in Carry On At Your Convenience cost £17.

815

Carry On Cabby was the first of Talbot Rothwell's script filmed as a Carry On, the first script he wrote was for Carry on Jack

816

Kenneth Williams wrote in his diary about Carry On Abroad: "Pinewood at 7.40. The first day, for me, of Carry On Abroad. If you'd told me in '58 that I'd still be coming out to Pinewood to make these films I'd have said you were mad. Though it was the first day, there was an air of staleness over everything. A feeling of 'I have been here before' and I thought the acting standard was rather bad throughout."

817

Kenneth Connor was awarded the MBE (Member of the Order of the British Empire) in the 1991 Queen's Birthday Honours List for his services to drama

818

Kenneth Williams had this to say in his diary about Carry On Matron: "First day of Carry On Matron. It was a murderous scene with medical dictionary plus thermometer in my mouth & taking the pulse and remembering every bit of business and I buggered it completely. By the time it got to take seven I heard Gerald [Thomas, director] say to the cameramen 'Oh! let's keep that one and print it... it won't get any better...' and of course he was right."

819

The nudist film in Carry On Camping is Nudist Paradise (1959).

820

Carry On Regardless had the most filmed material cut from the final film in the series.

821

Terry Scott was 42 when he made Carry On up The Jungle. His parents in the film were Joan Sims age 39 and Charles Hawtrey age 55.

822

Sid James and Barbara Windsor learned their dance routine in Carry On Henry just before filming, and completed it in one take.

823

The television special, Carry On Christmas, shown on ITV on Christmas Eve in 1969 had 18 million viewers.

824

Barbara Windsor lost weight before Carry On Again Doctor. This annoyed director Gerald Thomas as it ruined a joke about her character advertising Bristol's Bouncing Baby Food.

825

Max Harris composed the music for Carry On England. Regular Carry On composer Eric Rogers suggested him.

826

Peter Rogers was called 'Filthy Rich Rogers' by many of the Carry On cast.

827

Hattie Jacques appeared in Carry On Cabby, then missed seven Carry Ons before returning in Carry On Doctor.

828

Kenneth Williams wrote this in his diary about Carry On Doctor, while on a cruise ship holiday: "They are showing Carry On Doctor in the ship's cinema today at 5 o'c . They had it coming out as well! I'm staying in the cabin. See enough of my face in the mirror every day."

829

Phil Silvers wore his traditional horn rim glasses and had some lines to camera in Follow That Camel.

830

Gerald Thomas was a film editor before becoming a director. Like producer Peter Rogers, Thomas made sure he earned a percentage of the profits from the Carry On films as well as a flat fee so continued to make money from them throughout his life.

831

Sid James missed two Carry On films once – Carry On Jack in 1963 and Carry On Spying in 1964.

832

Richard O'Callaghan said he saw Carry On At Your Convenience a few years after it was released and "was embarrassed by it." He thought it was right wing and presented trade unionists in a bad light.

833

Kenneth Williams wrote this in his diary about Carry On Spying: "This is the first picture I've done the 'snide' voice in. I just hope it works."

834

The opening shot of Carry On Jack is a recreation of Arthur William Devis's famous painting The Death of Nelson, 21 October 1805. The painting can be seen in National Maritime Museum in Greenwich, London.

835

Carry On Regardless was inspired by a real employment agency called Universal Aunts which provided any service.

836

Peter Rogers had this to say about Carry On Cruising: "The most important member of the cast was the title "Carry On...", I would not allow anybody to go above it. The press said at the time if it didn't have Charles Hawtrey in it, it would not be worth seeing. This of course went straight to his head a bit, so his agent asked for more money, wanted to be the star, and have a star on his dressing room door. It was all rather silly, so we didn't use him".

837

There were rumours that Barbara Windsor and Sid James were dropped from Carry On Behind as they were too old to plat their usual Carry On roles. But, they were unavailable due to other work.

838

Director Gerald Thomas was very relaxed on set and was very fond of practical jokes.

839

Kenneth Williams had this to say in his diary about Carry On Again Doctor:

"To the Metropole to see Carry On Again Doctor. It was very good indeed, and should have got excellent reviews from the press. It moves along at a spanking pace, the cutting is excellent and the situations all hold. My performance as Carver, the surgeon, is remarkably authoritative and the incredibly banal lines which I have to say are made quite acceptable by the sort of style and panache I bring to the role. I was surprised and pleased, save for the fact that the greying hair was quite noticeably at times. Alas! my youth has left me. This should be the last film I do."

840

Julian Holloway said this about his cut scenes in Carry On Camping:

"I had some scenes in that film with Trisha Noble, we had a lot of romance scenes that ended up on the cutting room floor. Take the part at the end of the film with the goat, it makes absolutely no sense because the additional scenes with the goat were cut. I was supposed to rescue Trisha from the shower block from this man-eating goat as it traps her in there. If they had left that in it would have made slightly more sense with the end scene where it chases Amelia Bayntun."

841

Peter Rogers said that when he first me Frankie Howerd, Rogers had hurt his leg. Howerd suggested Rogers had fallen over his wallet.

842

Director Gerald Thomas was skilled at working with a small budget. He was creative when using locations and making sure there were limited takes and the films were made on schedule.

843

Barbara Windsor was not available for Carry On Behind as she was in New Zealand with her stage show Carry On Barbara.

844

The Carry On producers registered the title 'Carry on Charlie' for a proposed Carry On about Bonnie Prince Charlie.

845

Jack Douglas said his role as Sergeant Jock Strapp in Carry On Dick was his favourite.

846

Carry On producer Peter Rogers was declared bankrupt in 1994 after a failed investment in a television company. But when he died in 2009 he left £3.5 million in his will to charity.

847

Dora was offered the role of nurse Stella Dawson in Carry On Nurse. The role went to Joan Sims.

848

Julian Holloway appears in a Carry On for a first time in Follow That Camel as a train conductor.

849

Peter Rogers said this about the Carry Ons: "They were all alike, weren't they? We made 31 films out of one gag."

850

Kenneth Williams said that he earned more in a St Ivel butter television advert in 1980 than for any Carry On film.

851

Charles Hawtrey had a unique acting style in the films and would talk to the camera. He had his own style, trademark glasses and laugh.

852

Laurence Olivier once met Charles Hawtrey and said he should not be doing the Carry Ons.

853

Patricia Franklin appears in five Carry On films: Carry On Girls, Carry On Camping, Carry On Loving, Carry On Carry On Behind and England.

854

Peter Rogers famously said this about the Carry On cast: "I'll do anything for my actors, except pay them."

855

Carry On composer Eric Rogers and producer Peter Rogers were close friends sharing a love of music. But they were not related.

856

Jack Douglas did not like the last three Carry On films - which he appeared in. He thought Carry On England, Carry On Emmnauelle and Carry On Columbus "deviated from the Carry On formula".

857

Barbara Windsor was born Babara Deeks and chose her stage name Windsor after the Royal Family.

858

Kenneth Williams had this to say about Carry On Abroad in his diary:

"We saw the Carry On Abroad film which was made in '72 & I noticed that there were quite a few cuts! It wasn't all that bad considering the circumstances but the cast reminded one how unlovely the actors were. Not a dish to be seen. Kenny Connor was wonderfully diverting: he always has something singular to offer & this performance was delightful. Nobody else was v. good, apart from Joan Sims in the bed sequence and the pub, both v. authentic. I was all faces & jerks and old looking. The only think (ironically) I did that was funny was manipulate the exploding switchboard."

859

It was planned for Barbara Windsor to appear as a nurse at the end of Carry On Emmanuelle. But she had other work during filming.

860

Hattie Jacques was nicknamed Mother Superior on the Carry On set as she helped the cast with their problems.

861

Hattie Jacques had long grey hair and wore a wig in the Carry Ons.

862

Terence Longdon had the offer of a long term contract in the Carry On series, but Carry On Regardless was his last as he dd not want to commit to the series.

863

Carry On producer Peter Rogers was mean with his money, but did treat himself to a new Rolls Royce every year.

864

Kenneth Williams and Sid James did not get on on the Carry On set. Williams did not think James was a good actor, and James found Williams annoying with his attention seeking behaviour.

865

During rehearsals for the Carry On Laughing television series, Barbara Windsor dressed in a shawl, glasses and grey wig. No one recognised her, but thought her performance was very good. She then revealed that she was Barbara Windsor. She did not use the old lady outfit in the series though.

866

Hattie Jacques, famous for her roles as Matron in the Carry Ons, was a Red Cross nurse during World War 2.

867

Barbara Windsor appears in the tenth most number of Carry On films, and also appears in ten Carry Ons.

868

Jim Dale was asked to appear in the 1973 Carry On Christmas television show. He could not appear and his role went to Julian Holloway.

869

Producer Peter Rogers saw Peter Gilmore in the late 1950s television series Ivanhole with Roger Moore; he thought that Gilmore would be good in the Carry Ons.

870

Kenneth Williams and his mother and sister went with Barbara Windsor and Ronnie Knight on their honeymoon in Madeira

871

Jon Pertwee, who appears in four Carry Ons, called the Carry On series "hideous".

872

Bernard Bresslaw played a character from another race and used make up to play a Native American in Carry On Cowboy, an Arab in Follow That Camel and an African in Carry On Up The Jungle.

873

Carry On London went into pre-production in 2009. Charlie Higson was signed on to direct. The cast included Paul O'Grady, Lenny Henry, Justin Lee Collins, Jennifer Ellison and Frank Skinner. Sets were constructed at Pinewood Studios. But the filming never started and the project was abandoned after the death of Peter Rogers in 2009.

874

The Carry On films were dubbed into foreign languages. Sid James spoke of hearing his voice dubbed into Spanish:

"We were somewhere in Spain... and we saw Carry On Cowboy advertised. We thought we'd go and see it. There I was playing the Rumpo Kid... and they'd stuck a bloody soprano voice on me. The fella had a very high-pitched voice and a very high-pitched laugh. I nearly fell about. I stayed for about 10 minutes and then I couldn't stand it any longer. I had to get out of there. Fancy putting a voice like that on me!"

875

When Jim Dale did his own stunts on the Carry Ons, he was told to look at the camera so it was clear to the audience that it was Dale and not a stuntman.

876

Brian Oulton appears in Carry On Nurse, Carry On Cleo, Cleo, Carry On Constable and Carry On Camping.

He also appeared in the 1972 TV Christmas special Carry On Stuffing.

877

Jim Dale did not like dressing up as a French prostitute in Carry On Spying as the high heeled shoes were extremely uncomfortable.

878

It is reported in many Carry On guides that Cyril Chamberlain had a role in Carry On Spying, but he did not.

879

Before being cast in her first Carry On film, Carry On Spying, Barbara Windsor said he was a fan of the Carry On series and Kenneth Williams.

880

Carry On Spying went over budget by £11000. This was due to a number of on set accidents. The film ran over schedule and the actors had to be paid more money.

881

Carry On Girls was inspired by Miss World in 1970 which saw host Bob Hope pelted with tomatoes by feminist protesters.

882

When the filming of Carry On Spying switched to black and white, scenes were rewritten to pay homage to 1940s black and white noir films.

883

Valerie Leon said that Carry On Up The Jungle was her favourite Carry On film.

884

It was planned to have Stanley looking for Dr Livingstone in Carry On Up The Jungle, but the idea was scrapped.

885

Norman Hudis was asked to write a script for Carry On Spying, but producer Peter Rogers did not like it. Talbot Rothwell was asked to write a script, and this was used for the film.

886

June and Ug's English house at the end of Carry On Up The Jungle is the same house that Yoki the chimp's owner lived in in Carry On Regardless.

887

Leslie Phillips said Carry On Nurse was the funniest film he was in.

888

It is said that Terry Scott ignored his stunt double Billy Cornelius on the set of Carry On Up The Jungle.

889

Nina Baden-Semper appears as the female Nosha in Walter's

story in Carry On Up The Jungle..

890

Heather Emmanuel stars as a pregnant Lubi-Dubi in Carry On Up The Jungle.

891

Angela Douglas was going to play Jane in Carry On Up The Jungle. But she was decided to take a break from films after having a baby.

892

Bungdit Din's palace in Carry On Up The Khyber shares an exterior with Baron Bomburst's castle in Chitty Chitty Bang Bang.

893

On the set of Carry On Up The Khyber, Kenneth Williams ignored Wanda Ventham.

894

Paula's glasses in Carry On Girls were Valerie Leon's. She wore them when working at Harrods.

895

In Carry On Girls Phillip Webb plays two characters: a council member and a man on the Tube.

896

Ed Devereaux appears in five Carry On films: Carry On Sergeant, Carry On Nurse, Carry On Jack, Carry On Regardless, and Carry On Cruising.

897

On the back of a VHS edition of Carry On Girls Mayor Bumble is called Major Bumble.

898

Jimmy Logan said that his role as Cecil Gaybody in Carry On Girls was embarrassing and he was ashamed of it.

899

Patsy Rowlands appears in nine Carry On films:

Carry On Again Doctor, Carry On Loving, Carry On Henry, Carry On At Your Convenience, Carry On Matron (1972), Carry On Abroad (1972), Carry On Girls (1973) Carry On Dick (1974) and Carry On Behind (1975).

She also appeared in the Carry On Laughing television show.

900

Terence Longden's part in Carry On Regardless was written for Leslie Phillips; Phillips declined as he did not want to typecast as a "silly ass".

901

In Carry On Teacher, Shelia and Irene Dale were played by real life sisters Carol and Jane White

902

In Carry On Up the Khyber when Burpa cannons are fired at the Residency, Bungdit Din (Bernard Bresslaw) says "that'll teach them to ban turbans on the buses". This was a reference to Sikh bus drivers who were striking over not being allowed to wear turbans on buses in Britain.

903

Fircombe in Carry On Girls was originally called Bungcope – pronounced "bunk up".

904

In Carry On Doctor there us a portrait of James Robertson Justice on a wall. There is a caption next to it saying "Dr James R. Justice, Founder". This refers to the Doctor series of comedy films, which starred James Robertson Justice.

905

In Carry On Girls, the photographer was supposed to be a non speaking role. But Sid James had starred with Robin Askwith in the comedy film Bless this house and asked that Askwith be cast. Askwith's role as Larry Prodworthy was expanded.

906

Kenneth Williams and Terry Scott thought of Cromwell and

Cardinal Wolsey's last lines of "Carry on, executioner!" in Carry On Henry.

907

Patsy Rowlands was critical of her performance in Carry On Henry believing it to be too straight.

908

In Carry On Loving, Sid says "Alright?" when he sees the lovers kissing in the lift. The original line was "going up?", but the censors would not allow it.

909

Kenneth Williams wrote this about Carry On up The Jungle in his diary in 1976: "In the evening I stayed in to watch Carry On Up The Jungle which was a Carry On which I didn't appear in. It was quite funny and at one point I was laughing along. I was staggered to see what they got away with!! A snake going up the skirt of Joan Sims! & her look of horror turning to delight!! Kenny Connor was quite marvelous, and Terry Scott was excellent as Tarzan.".

910

Carry On Henry started development in 1966 was finally filmed in 1971.

911

Gertan Klauber appears in seven Carry On films: Carry On Cleo, Carry On Spying, Carry On Doctor, Carry On Henry, Carry On Abroad, Carry On Emmannuelle and Carry On Follow

That Camel.

912

Patsy Rowlands had a long, dramatic scene as the Queen at her execution. But the scene was shortened, with director Gerald Thomas calling the scene "too dramatic".

913

Valerie Shute plays the girl lover in Carry On Loving who is seen kissing her boyfriend in numerous locations. She had to do several takes of the scene where her character has a cream cake thrown on her face and ended up with irritating the skin on her face and a dislike of cream cakes.

914

Richard O'Callaghan appears for the first time on Carry On Loving. He said that before he was cast he was a fam of the older Carry On such as Carry On Sergeant and Carry On Cabby.

915

A planned scene in Carry On Loving where Kenneth Williams's character Percival Snopper put his hand in through a window was dropped from the film. This is because Williams thought he would hurt himself, even though the glass was only made of sugar. Director Gerald Thomas put his hand through some of the sugar glass to persuade Kenneth it was safe - and cut his hand.

916

Rosalind Knight appears in two Carry On films: Carry On

Nurse and Carry On Teacher.

917

In Carry On Matron, when Kenneth Cope played a female nurse he had a female stand in for some scenes.

918

Peter Butterworth was cast as Freddy in Carry On Loving. But he had other work commitments so Bill Maynard took the role

919

Nicholas Parsons hated the suit wore in Carry On Regardless because it didn't fit him properly.

920

The original character names for Kenneth Williams and Charles Hawtrey in Carry On Abroad were Kenneth Stuart-Farquhar and Charles Makepeace.

921

In Carry On Abroad Danid Kernan is Nicholas who is straight and admired by his gay friend Rob, played by John Clive. In real life Kernan was gay and Clive was straight.

922

Amanda Barrie appears in two Carry On films: Carry On Cabby and Carry On Cleo.

923

In the opening scene of Carry On Screaming! Albert courts Doris who is frightened. Angela Douglas kept screaming louder in each take, which annoyed Jim Dale.

924

Captain Ryan's transformation into a werewolf in the 2002 film Dog Soldiers was inspired by Carry On Screaming.

925

Vincent Price was asked to appear in Carry On Screaming!, but he asked £25,000 so the idea was abandoned.

926

Deborah Kerr was asked to play Valeria in Carry On Screaming! for a large fee, but she chose to appear in a stage play instead.

927

Carry On producer Peter Rogers said this about the success of the Carry On series:

"When we first hit the jackpot with Sergeant. well that's one thing, perhaps a lucky fluke everyone said but when we did it again with Nurse only bigger the producer used to say to me, 'Oh Peter, now you can make an epic if you want to, you can write your own ticket'. I said, 'I don't want to make any bloody epics. I want to stay in my own backyard and make another Carry On'.

928

Fenella Fielding's dress in Carry On Screaming! Was too small and very uncomfortable; she could not even sit down in it.

929

In 1998, British television channel Channel 4 made a documentary about the "dark" side of four Carry On stars: Sid James, Kenneth Williams, Charles Hawtrey and Frankie Howerd. This showed the so called dark side of the actors by with details about their lives that most people already knew about.

930

In Carry On Abroad, Rob and Nicholas were initially supposed to be boyfriends. But the censors did not like this and the script was changed to have Nicholas falling in love with Lily and Rob to simply be gay who is attracted to his friend.

931

Angela Douglas did not like her mannequin in Carry On Screaming! as it made her neck look too big.

932

At the end of Carry On Spying, Dilys Laye says Kenneth Williams's catchphrase "stop messing about" at Kenneth. It was an ad lib.

933

The striped blazer worn Kenneth Williams In Carry On

Camping is worn by Kenneth Connor in Carry On Abroad.

934

Carry On Again Doctor has three different plots. This is a result of the script being revised several times before filming.

935

Phil Silvers received a £30,000 fee, first class air travel and a limousine for Carry On Follow That Camel.

936

Scenes of the cast on the plane were cut from Carry On Abroad to avoid the cost of building a new set.

937

In Carry On Teacher, all the actors playing the children in the orchestra could really play their own instruments. for example, Richard O'Sullivan was a very good piano player.

938

When Carry On Again Doctor was shown on British television station ITV3 in 2021 the word crumpet was cut out.

939

In Carry On Dick, Sid is twice the age of the real Dick Turpin.

940

In Carry On Abroad, it was originally planned to have Elsbels located on the Costa Bomm.

941

In early drafts of the Carry On Camping script, a character called Rosemary lost her bra in the exercise scene and not Barbara Windsor's Babs.

942

In Carry On at Your Convenience Tina Hart plays an usherette and a dancer.

943

The role of Montgomery Infield-Hopping in Carry On Regardless was written for Leslie Phillips. But Phiilips did not want the role, complaining of typecasting. The role went to Terence Longdon.

944

Screenwriter made fun of Charles Hawtrey by depicting him Carry On Abroad as an alcoholic, camp and a Mummy's Boy. This is what Hawtrey was lie in real life.

945

Carry On At Your Convenience had fifty minutes of footage cut from the film

946

The town sets built for Carry On Follow That Camel were used for Carry On Up the Khyber.

947

Kenneth Williams did not like Elke Summer during filming of Carry On Behind.

948

Julian Holoway had this to say about the payment of the Carry On actors:

"No question about it. [producer Peter] Rogers always used to say that the title 'Carry On' was the star, that was just a cosy way of him getting off paying us big money. Take poor Joan Sims. I understand that she died virtually destitute – that should never have happened. Had we been in America and have had the Screen Actors Guild it would have been very different. We even went to Equity in the 1960's. It took them another 30 years to make the changes [in Britain] to protect actors in a similar position. They didn't make the changes until 1993. "

949

There is a 1937 comedy film called Carry On London, but it is unreleated to the Carry On series.

950

The British censors wanted to censor the scenes of the stripper's bare breast in the opening projection scenes of Carry On Behind. Another scene where Linda Upmore's breasts are viewed "dangling" from a caravan. The censor from the British Board of Film Classification john Trevelyan was retiring after checking most of the Carry On films.: he left the scenes in Carry On Behind as a gift.

951

Carry On Cabby was Hattie Jacques's favourite Carry On because in it she plays a warmer character rather than a stern one.

952

On back of the 2005 of an Australian DVD release of Carry On Camping by by Magna Pacific, Joan Sims's character is called Esme Crowfoot. This is the name of her character in Carry On Loving; in Carry On |Camping she is Joan Fussey.

953

Original Carry On writer Norman Hudis wrote a script for Carry On Again Nurse in 1988. For the cast Hudis wanted Kenneth Williams as Sir Roderick Haddon, Joan Sims as Matron Millicent Bullivant, Charles Hawtrey as Cecil Cholmondeley, Kenneth Connor as Harry Drummond, and Barbara Windsor as Sister H. Chesterton. Unfortunately the film was not made as Kenneth Williams and Charles Hawtrey died in 1988.

954

Lawrie Wyman and George Evans wrote an initial script for Carry On Dick where Dick Turpin was called Dick Twerpin

955

The hippy dancing sequence at the end of Carry On Camping was filmed on the 5th and 6th of November 1968.

956

Carry On scriptwriter Norman Hudis wrote a Carry On film for the 30th anniversary of the Carry On series in 1988. The film was called Carry On Again Nurse the film was based in a hospital threatened with cuts. The producers struggled to raise the £1.5 million budget and the film was not made. Charles Hawtrey and Kenneth Williams died in 1988, so the year would not have been a good time for a Carry On.

957

Fenella Fielding was asked to appear in Carry On Camping. She turned down the offer as she did not like the script.

958

The British Board for Film Censorship censored some lines from the Carry On Dick script. Lines included "I am far too busy to worry about how I am hung" and " there's nothing like an old mare for a comfortable ride".

959

The proposed, but unmade, Carry On London in production between 2003-2009 had many actors liked with it such as Burt Reynolds, Shaun Williamson, Vinnie Jones, Shane Ritchie, Paul O'Grady, Lenny Henry, Frank Skinner and Jennifer Ellison. Peter Richardson and Charlie Higson were mentioned as directors.

960

Sally Geeson, appears in Carry On Girls and Carry On Abroad. She also appears in Carry On Regardless aged 11 in an unaccredited role.

961

Julian Holloway said that he was "overwhelmed with work" during the filming of Carry On Camping as he was also appearing in a play in the evening.

962

Hattie Jacques was hoped to appear in a cameo role as the Matron at the maternity hospital but was too busy starring in Sykes. Brenda Cowling then took her place.

963

Julian Holloway said this about Carry On England:

"By that stage Rogers [producer Peter Rogers] was trying to compete with the 'Confessions' films and it was pathetic. We had gone from seaside postcard to full down and dirty.

964

Valerie Van Ost appears in four Carry Ons: Cary On Cabby, Carry On Don't Lose Your Head, Carry On Doctor, and Carry On Again Doctor.

965

Melvyn Hayes had this to say about Carry On England:

"It was the worst one made! It was a dreadful film."

966

Some scenes of the holidaymakers onbard a plane were cut from the script of Carry On Abroad before filming. These scenes included:

Cora being scared of flying; Vic being sick; Mr. Farquhar missing Miss Plunkett's obvious flirting; Brother Bernard retrieving Marge's handbag for her.; Evelyn insisting on a separate room from Stanley at the hotel; Stanley pinching the hostess' bottom.; Mr. Tuttle showing Bert one of his clients in an adult magazine; Rob telling Nicholas of the one time he had been out with a girl and Sadie lying to Bert that she had accidentally killed her husband with rat poison.

967

Gail Grainger had this to say about her role in Carry On Abroad:

"They also wanted a total contrast to Barbara's character. I think everyone thought that the part would be offered to Valerie Leon as she was of a similar character. I don't know why, but she wasn't cast."

968

Julian Holloway said Kenneth Williams told him to not make any more Carry Ons after Carry On Camping. Williams said: "Don't let the stigma of the Carry On's attach itself to you".

969

Gertan Klauber was cast in several Carry on when a sinister of big, cheerful character was needed.

970

Billy Cornelius had this to say about his role in Carry On Screaming and his Oddjob makeup:

"It took an hour and a half. It took ages and it was very hot. I remember one day I had to also stand in for Tommy Clegg [who played Oddbod]. Tommy had contracted Asian flu and was unwell, so I ended up having to swap into his outfit and makeup too. I was shattered!"

971

The Censors wanted to give Carry On Girls a more adult AA certificate, but a few cuts gained it an A certificate.

972

Jack Douglas appears in eight Carry On films - the last eight films.

973

During the filming of Carry On Dick, Sid James, Barbara Windsor, Bernard Bresslaw, Kenneth Connor, Jack Douglas and Peter Butterworth were appearing in Carry On London on stage in London. They had two shows at 6.15 PM and 8.45 PM. They had to complete their filming for Carry On Dick at 4.15 PM each day.

974

Wilfred Bramble's performance in Carry On Again Doctor was filmed on 1st April 1969 and earned him £100.

975

Eric Rogers' brother Alan Rogers wrote the saloon song This Is The Time For Love in Carry On Cowboy.

976

Carry On Constable was going to be called Carry On Copper, but it was thought this would be disrespectful.

977

Producer Peter Rogers said the first day filming a new Carry On was like the first day back at school, because of the regular cast and crew.

978

During Jim Dale's scene at the hospital dance in Carry On Again Doctor, Eric Rogers includes bits of score from Dale's other Carry On scenes: from Carry On Cabby and the Carry On Spying song.

979

For Carry On Columbus, producer John Goldstone upset many fans by saying that that even if Sid James, Kenneth Williams and Hattie Jacques had been alive they would have been to old to be cast.

980

There were two versions of Carry On England. One featured topless scenes and a Fokker joke. The other cut these out. Both versions were on the DVD release, but the VHS had the cut version.

981

In 1972 Peter Rogers asked Dave Freeman to write a non Carry On comedy script. It was a caravan holiday themed comedy called Love On Wheels. In 1974 Rogers asked Freeman to adapt it for a Carry On, and it became Carry On Behind.

982

Peter Rogers had this to say about composer Eric Rogers:

"..he was a good craftsman, he knew a lot about music, but if you understand me, he didn't know a lot of music, particularly classical music. For instance, in Carry On Matron, in one of the hospital scenes, Gwen Watford was waddling down the corridor heavily pregnant. Eric said, 'What on earth do we do for that'. I said, 'Well you know there's a piece of music in the Pictures From An Exhibition called the Ballet of the Unhatched Chicks', I said, 'Let's use that'. So it was a little joke between us, I don't know if anybody got it."

983

Charles Hawtrey pulled out of the 1972 Carry On Christmas television show. His role was split between Brian Oulton and Norman Rossington.

984

Bob Monkhouse appears in Carry On Sergeant, the first Carry On. He turned down more Carry On parts, choosing other comedy films.

985

Peter Rogers said he has never seen a Carry On film:

"I've never seen one. I don't look at them. It's not because I don't want to but you see, I never saw them in London, I never saw a preview or anything. Once they left the studio here, I said to Gerald, 'Leave them alone, don't start fiddling with them. That's what we think they should be and that's what it's going to be".

986

Lindsay Marsh was hired to play an air hostess in Carry On Abroad and paid even though she did not film any scenes.

987

In 1995, producer Peter rogers said that he would never watch any of the Carry On films. "What a punishment. Even the Marquis de Sade couldn't have devised a worse torture" he said!

988

Jack Douglas said the films were not demeaning to women:

"It was always the ladies who came off best and Sid James who got the worst of the deal".

989

Kenneth Williams had this to say in his diary about Carry On Henry: "We saw the TV and it was Carry On Henry... amazing how well this was made! Everyone in it was competent and the sheer look of the thing was so professional."

990

Scriptwriter Norman Hudis was inspired for Carry On Nurse by his nurse wife Rita:

"I used to call downstairs to Rita and say 'put on the old nurse's cap and tell me something funny'."

991

Norman Hudis wrote Carry On scripts Carry On Under the Pier If Wet and Carry On Shylock Holmes but they were not used.

992

For Carry On Cleo, producer Peter Rogers and director Gerald Thomas were paid £7,500 each; Sidney James and Kenneth Williams received £5,000 each; Charles Hawtrey and writer Talbot Rothwell received £4,000; Jim Dale's got £1,000; Cleopatra Amanda Barrie received £550 and Joan Sims was employed on a daily basis of £125 per day.

993

There were rumours that Sid James and Barbara Windsor were dropped from Carry On Behind as they were too old for their traditional roles. But they were working outside Britain at the time the Carry On was filmed.

994

The nudist film shown in the cinema at the start of Carry On Camping was the first time female topless scenes appeared in the series.

995

Angela Douglas said she looks on all her Carry On films with affection.

996

In the original script for Carry On Girls, the film ended with a car chase and a wedding between Sid Fiddler and Hope Springs.

997

Angela Douglas recalled this scene in Carry On Cowboy:

I had to do a scene where I was wearing high heels, spangles, a low cut corset and I was a bag of nerves. Joan Sims gave me a small brandy and pushed me on set!"

998

Director Gerald Thomas was concerned about the scene in Carry On Up The Khyber where the soldiers life up their kilts as he thought it was not suitable for his children.

999

The 1959 nudist film shown at the start of Carry On Camping has contemporary topless scenes of Gilly Grant added.

1000

Charles Hawtrey appeared in 23 of the first 24 Carry On films.

He only missed Carry On Cruising.

Photo Credit:

2 August 2017

darrencoleshill

https://pixabay.com/photos/architecture-building-infrastructure-2566173/